50 DESIGNERS
YOU SHOULD KNOW

50 DESIGNERS
YOU SHOULD KNOW

Hajo Düchting
Claudia Hellmann
Nina Kozel
Marco Maurer
Johannes Rave
Josef Straßer
Annette Winkler

Prestel
Munich · London · New York

Front cover from top to bottom:
Arne Jacobsen, Ant Chairs, 1952
Marianne Brandt, MT 49 tea infuser, 1924, see p. 38
Verner Panton, Panton Chair, 1960, see p. 95
Le Corbusier, Pierre Jeanneret, and Charlotte Perriand, LC 4 chaise longe, 1928, see p. 30
Frontispiz: Alessi (Stefano Giovannoni), kettle SG 65 Mami
Seite 10/11: Karim Rashid, Metro station university, Naples, 2011

© Prestel Verlag, Munich · London · New York, 2012
© for the works reproduced is held by the artists, their heirs or assigns, with the exception of: Alvar Aaalto, Max Bill, Marianne Brandt, Walter Gropius, Ludwig Mies van der Rohe, Pierre Jeanneret, Charlotte Perriand, Jean Prouve, Gerrit Rietveld, Wilhelm Wagenfeld with VG Bild-Kunst, Bonn 2012; Le Corbusier with FLC / VG Bild-Kunst, Bonn 2012; Isamu Noguchi with The Isamu Noguchi Foundation and Garden Museum / VG Bild-Kunst, Bonn 2012; Ron Arad with Ron Arad; Edward Barber and Jay Osgerby with Jay Osgerby & Edward Barber; Ronan & Erwan Bouroullec with Ronan & Erwan Bouroullec; Achille Castiglioni with Achille Castiglioni Foundation; Terence Conran with Terence Conran; Lucienne and Robin Day with Robin and Lucienne Day Foundation; Tom Dixon with Tom Dixon; Charles and RayEames with Eames Foundation; Konstantin Grcic with Konstantin Grcic; Pierre Jeanneret with VG Bild-Kunst, Bonn 2012; Raymond Loewy with Raymond Loewy Foundation; Vico Magistretti with Fondazione Vico Magistretti; Ingo Maurer with Ingo Maurer; Jasper Morrison with Jasper Morrison; Marc Newson with Marc Newson; Verner Panton with Verner Panton Design, Basel; Andree Putman with Andrée Putman; Karim Rashid with Karim Rashid; Ettore Sottsass with Studio Ettore Sottsass; Philippe Starck with Philippe Starck; Tapio Wirkkala with Tapio Wirkkala-Rut Bryk Foundation

Prestel Verlag, Munich
A member of Verlagsgruppe Random House GmbH

Prestel Verlag
Neumarkter Strasse 28
81673 Munich
Tel. +49 (0)89 4136-0
Fax +49 (0)89 4136-2335

Prestel Publishing Ltd.
4 Bloomsbury Place
London WC1A 2QA
Tel. +44 (0)20 7323-5004
Fax +44 (0)20 7636-8004

Prestel Publishing
900 Broadway, Suite 603
New York, NY 10003
Tel. +1 (212) 995-2720
Fax +1 (212) 995-2733

www.prestel.com

Library of Congress Control Number is available; British Library Cataloguingin-Publication Data: a catalogue record for this book is available from the British Library; Deutsche Nationalbibliothek holds a record of this publication in the Deutsche Nationalbiblio grafie; detailed bibliographical data can be found under: http://dnb.d-nb.de

Prestel books are available worldwide. Please contact your nearest bookseller or one of the above addresses for information concerning your local distributor.

Project management: Claudia Stäuble, Franziska Stegmann
Translation: Katherine O'Donoghue
Copyediting: Danko Szabó
Picture research: Andrea Weißenbach, Utting am Ammersee
Timeline: Franziska Stegmann
Cover and design: LIQUID, Agentur für Gestaltung, Augsburg
Layout and production: zwischenschritt, Rainald Schwarz, Munich
Origination: ReproLine Mediateam
Druck und Bindung: Druckerei Uhl GmbH & Co. KG, Radolfzell

Verlagsgruppe Random House FSC®-DEU-0100
The FSC®-certified paper Hello Fat Matt has been
produced by mill Condat, Le Lardin Saint-Lazare, France.

Printed in Germany

ISBN 978-3-7913-4720-2

CONTENTS

1809 Charles Darwin is born

1745	1750	1755	1760	1765	1770	1775	1780	1785	1790	1795	1800	1805	1810	1815	1820	1825	1830	

Michael Thonet, coffeehouse
chair No. 214, re-edition by
Thonet GmbH

WILLIAM MORRIS

1837 Victoria becomes queen 1851 First World's Fair in London
of the United Kingdom

1874 First Impressionist
exhibition in Paris

1894 Tower Bridge in London
opened for traffic

1914 Beginning
of World
War I

1857 Gustave Flaubert,
Madame Bovary

1887–1889 Eiffel Tower
built in Paris

1900 Boxer Rebellion in China

1835 1840 1845 1850 1855 1860 1865 1870 1875 1880 1885 1890 1895 1900 1905 1910 1915 1920

MICHAEL THONET

"Never was a better and more elegant design and a more precisely crafted and practical item created." This was how the architect Le Corbusier admiringly described the bentwood furniture. It was a cabinetmaker from Boppard, a small town on the Rhine River, who revolutionized furniture design of the 19th century with his pioneering invention.

Around 1830, Michael Thonet began to experiment with a new process that permitted him to bend laminated wood and later even solid beech-wood rods into curved shapes using steam and pressure. With the bentwood, he broke new ground in design during the mechanical and industrial age.

The Austrian Chancellor Prince Klemens Wenzel von Metternich, who was himself from the Rhineland, was impressed by Thonet's work at the Koblenz trade fair in 1841. He advised Thonet to go to Vienna and promised to put in a good word for him at court. In 1842, Thonet was granted the privilege by the Imperial and Royal Court Chamber to "bend any type of wood, even the most brittle, into any shape or curve using chemical-mechanical methods." Thonet first worked for the parquet manufacturer Carl Leistler and created magnificent parquet floors and chairs for the Palais Liechtenstein. In 1849, he established his own workshop for the production of bentwood furniture, which, after 1853, was run under the name Gebrüder Thonet when he transferred the business to his five sons (without of course removing himself from the business).

In 1849, *Chair No. 1* was created for the garden palace of Prince Schwarzenberg. Its construction was revolutionary: the individual parts created from bentwood were all finished parts that could be combined with the parts of other models using a toolbox principle. Thonet thus created the basis for the variety of types and models in industrial mass production. The company's most successful model was *Chair No. 14*, which was made of solid beech and created in 1859. It became famous as a Viennese coffeehouse chair. Over 50 million units of this model alone were sold by 1930. It is the most manufactured chair in the world and is a perfect example of a modern article of mass consumption.

In the 1850s, Thonet established a flourishing bentwood furniture industry by moving the production sites to the forested regions of Moravia, Silesia, Hungary, and Poland and by increasing worldwide sales. This is where Thonet's true talent became apparent as he combined his groundbreaking invention with ingenious business sense. The bending of solid wood, which is what had made industrial mass production at all possible, was soon copied by competitors. Thonet's bentwood furniture was clearly identified by the stamp and trademarks and could be taken apart. The low transport costs made it perfect for export. Worldwide turnover was expanded with the aid of advertisements, catalogs, and retail outlets in all the major cities of Europe and the US.

The company continued to flourish even after Michael Thonet's death in 1871, and after the turn of the century, leading designers began to create furniture for Gebrüder Thonet. In 1929, the French subsidiary Thonet Frères was established and the product range was expanded to include tubular steel furniture by Marcel Breuer and Ludwig Mies van der Rohe, among others. The Thonet family business is now being run by the fifth generation and is today based in Frankenberg, in North Hessen, Germany. *ch*

1796 Born in Boppard am Rhein
1819 Establishes a furniture workshop in Boppard
1830 First experiments with bentwood (Boppard laminated wood chairs)
1842 Invited to Vienna by Prince Metternich
1843–1846 Works with his five sons at the parquet company Carl Leistler, including work on furnishings at the Palais Liechtenstein
1849 Establishes his own furniture workshop in Vienna, run from 1853 on under the name Gebrüder Thonet
1851 Bronze medal for Thonet's furniture at the first World's Fair, London
1856 Patents the process for bending solid wood
1859 *Chair No. 14* (Viennese coffeehouse chair)
1860 Establishes factory production
1867 Awarded the gold medal at the World's Fair in Paris
1871 Dies in Vienna

Portrait of Michael Thonet

above
Gebrüder Thonet, Chair No. 209,
re-edition by Thonet GmbH

right page
Gebrüder Thonet, Chair No. 233,
re-edition by Thonet GmbH

1805 Battles of Trafalgar
and Austerlitz

1830 July Revolution in France

1855 Courbet's *Réalism* exhibition

1797 Invention of lithography

1861–1865 American
Civil War

1785 1790 1795 1800 1805 1810 1815 1820 1825 1830 1835 1840 1845 1850 1855 1860 1865 1870

1901 Queen Victoria dies

1897 Tate Gallery is founded
in London

1914 Marcel Duchamp's first
readymade, *Bottle Rack*

1939–1945 World War II

1947 India gains independence
from the British Empire

1875 1880 1885 1890 1895 1900 1905 1910 1915 1920 1925 1930 1935 1940 1945 1950 1955 1960

WILLIAM MORRIS

As the founder of the Arts and Crafts movement, William Morris was one of the most influential designers of the 19th century, his reformist ideas having had a major influence on the start of the modern age.

The Arts and Crafts movement originated in England in the 19th century and represented a protest against industrialization, which produced only poor quality and unattractive, sterile results. Its representatives, in particular William Morris, wanted to find an authentic style for the 19th century and they rejected the overloaded, bulky furniture that was common at the time. Its objective was to return to the simpler shapes and traditional manufacturing processes of craftwork, away from the inhumane factories.

The most famous works of William Morris include the floral wallpaper designs that were also used in textiles and, in a simplified form, in carpets. He used nature as the inspiration for these designs. It was not just the appropriate counterpart to industrialism, which he rejected, but for the religious Morris, it also represented the perfect design as it had been designed by God. With his wallpaper, Morris succeeded in bringing a piece of nature into the home. His patterns were always stylized plants, mainly flowers, and included the names of the plants shown. The wallpaper designs by Morris are still sold today under license by the London companies Sanderson and Liberty.

William Morris was, however, much more than just a creative and talented wallpaper designer. He worked as a painter, architect, poet, craftsman, engineer, and publisher, and was a passionate aesthete and one of England's first socialists. He developed his great interest in art, architecture, and design during his theology studies, when he became familiar with the Pre-Raphaelite movement. He was particularly fascinated by the Gothic movement. As a wedding present for his wife, he and his friends Edward Burne-Jones and Dante Gabriel Rossetti furnished her house, the Red House, taking inspiration from nature and from the Middle Ages. They subsequently formed the cooperative Morris, Marshall, Faulkner & Co. Thus their hobby became a company that, from 1861 on, manufactured furniture and other decorative objects such as ceramics, stained glass, wallpaper, metal goods, tiles, materials, and embroideries in accordance with their ideals of simplicity, craftwork, and usefulness. In 1874, he took on the management of the workshops alone and expanded them. Morris employed many talented artists and artisans and always categorically rejected industrial production. At the end of the 1880s, Morris experienced an identity crisis. His idea that the Arts and Crafts movement would reform society had not been achieved. Instead of changing mechanical mass production, the popularity of his products in fact meant that they were being copied by the factories.

Although William Morris did not achieve his goal of producing good, crafted products for the masses, he was, with his ideals, still a mastermind of the modern age. With his floral designs and the return to nature, he was a pioneer of Art Nouveau. His vision of creating good design for all and the rejuvenation of handicrafts also influenced the German Werkbund artist association and the Bauhaus school. *nk*

1834 Born on March 24 in Waltham-
stow, Essex, Great Britain
1853 Studies theology in Oxford
1856 Works in the architecture agency
G. E. Street
1859 Marries Jane Burden
1861 Establishes the cooperative
Morris, Marshall, Faulkner & Co
1877 Establishes the Society for the
Protection of Ancient Buildings
1891 Establishes the Kelmscott Press
for manufacturing high-quality
books
1896 Dies in London

left page
William Morris, *Strawberry Thief*
wallpaper, circa 1897

above
Portrait of William Morris

WILLIAM MORRIS

JOSEF HOFFMANN

1848–1849 Revolutions in
numerous European
countries

1861–1865 American
Civil War

1888 Vincent van Gogh,
Sunflowers

| 1820 | 1825 | 1830 | 1835 | 1840 | 1845 | 1850 | 1855 | 1860 | 1865 | 1870 | 1875 | 1880 | 1885 | 1890 | 1895 | 1900 | 1905 |

Glasgow School of Art

1911 Marie Curie awarded the Nobel Prize for Chemistry

1927 Charles Lindbergh flies nonstop from New York to Paris

1939–1945 World War II

1955 *The Family of Man* exhibition at MoMA in New York

1973 Yom Kippur War

1978 The Galápagos Islands are the first item on the UNESCO World Heritage list

1989 Fall of the Berlin Wall

1910 1915 1920 1925 1930 1935 1940 1945 1950 1955 1960 1965 1970 1975 1980 1985 1990 1995

CHARLES RENNIE MACKINTOSH

He was committed to the Arts and Crafts movement and at the same time had a rather unique, distinctive style. Many of his projects — the Glasgow School of Art, the decoration of tea shops in his Scottish hometown — were developed with the notion of a complete work of art. Today, he is primarily known for his striking chair designs.

Paris, Vienna, Brussels — at the end of the 19th and start of the 20th centuries, these were the centers of the artistic avant-garde movement. The Scottish architect and designer Charles Rennie Mackintosh, who during his lifetime remained closely linked to his hometown — the emerging industrial metropolis of Glasgow — worked away from these classical art centers. In spite of this, or maybe because of this, he quickly made his name as an architect and furniture designer with his works, whose highly individual shapes — first organic, then strictly geometric — had a major influence on the style of the fin de siècle.

The most outstanding work by the architect is probably the new Glasgow School of Art, which was constructed from 1896 to 1899, and which he expanded ten years later with the construction of a library. As a young man, he had attended evening classes in drawing and painting here himself while he worked as an apprentice for the architecture company run by John Hutchinson. The new building of the art school was captivating with its formal clear lines and its interior design, which was planned to the smallest detail and which included matching furniture.

Together with the painter and glass artist Margaret MacDonald, who would later become his wife, her sister Frances MacDonald McNair, and her husband, James Herbert McNair — all students of the Glasgow School of Art — Mackintosh formed the group "The Four." They represented art influenced by the Scottish Arts and Crafts movement and included references from Celtic and Japanese art in their geometric style, the so-called Glasgow Style. Mackintosh was particularly fascinated by the simple shapes of Japanese architecture and was inspired by them in his reduced interiors, which were identified by geometric ornaments and flooded with light. The harmonious union of the most diverse contrasts — modern and traditional, black and white, vertical and horizontal — characterizes many of his projects.

Mackintosh achieved international fame and recognition after he accepted the invitation from Josef Hoffmann in 1900 to take part in the exhibition of the Vienna Secession. His geometric style, his integrated approach, and projects that were often designed as complete works of art were echoed in the German and Austrian design of this time. Whether in the Glasgow School of Art, in Hill House, or in the Glasgow tea rooms designed by him, Mackintosh did not take responsibility for just the architecture; he also designed the walls, furniture, textiles, and other details. Between 1887 and 1905, for example, he designed more than 400 pieces of furniture, in particular chairs in the austere style, such as the *Argyle* model (1898) and the *Willow 1* chair (1904), which was influenced by Japanese shapes, for the Willow Road Tea Rooms. The most famous is probably the *Hill House* model (1903) with its dramatically high backrests and the black-painted, solid wood construction that were typical for Mackintosh and that Mackintosh designed for the eponymous villa of the publisher W. W. Blackie. *ch*

1868 Born in Glasgow, Scotland
1884 Apprentice to the architect John Hutchinson in Glasgow
1889–1913 Works at the architecture company Honeyman & Keppie in Glasgow
1891 Traveling scholarship through Europe
1896–99 Construction of the Glasgow School of Art
1896–97 Designs the interior for the Glasgow tea rooms
1900 Marries Margaret MacDonald; participates in the Vienna Secession exhibition
1902–04 Hill House in Helensburgh to the north of Glasgow
1907–09 Expansion of the Glasgow School of Art by the addition of a library
1923 Moves to Port Vendres, France, and devotes himself to painting
1928 Dies in London

Portrait of Charles Rennie Mackintosh

left page
Charles Rennie Mackintosh, Hill House Chair, 1904–08

right
Willow Chair, 1917

1826 First photograph by
Joseph Nicéphore Niépce

1837 Victoria becomes queen
of the United Kingdom

1848 Karl Marx and Friedrich Engels
publish the *Communist Manifesto*

1855 Courbet's *Réalism*
exhibition

1869–1883 Construction of the Brooklyn
Bridge in New York

1870/71 Franco-Prussian War

1897 Auguste Rodin,
Balzac

1820	1825	1830	1835	1840	1845	1850	1855	1860	1865	1870	1875	1880	1885	1890	1895	1900	1905

1921 Arnold Schoenberg invents
twelve-tone music

905 German Expressionist group Die Brücke
is founded in Dresden

1939 Germany invades Poland;
World War II commences

1914 Beginning of World War I

1910 1915 1920 1925 1930 1935 1940 1945 1950 1955 1960 1965 1970 1975 1980 1985 1990 1995

JOSEF HOFFMANN

Josef Hoffmann was one of the most influential artistic figures at the start of the 20th century. As a founding member of the Wiener Werkstätte, Hoffmann played a significant role in the development of modern art in Vienna.

As a member of the Viennese Secession, the Austrian architect and designer played a key role in the development of a modern art concept. With Koloman Moser, he was also a founding member and one of the main representatives of the Wiener Werkstätte (1903–32), a group of architects and designers who strove to rejuvenate arts and crafts. The products were to be characterized by their individuality, beauty, and precise design. With his functionally strict yet decorative and inventive furniture designs, Hoffmann also became one of the most influential furniture designers of modern times.

From 1887 on, Josef Hoffmann attended the Höhere Staatsgewerbeschule in Brno, where he learned the principles of antique architecture, in particular of Greek architecture and the Italian Renaissance. After a year of practical experience as a construction trainee in Würzburg, Hoffmann began his studies at the Academy of Fine Arts in Vienna. Hoffmann has Otto Wagner (1841–1918) in particular to thank for the important insights into modern architecture. After Hoffmann joined the Vienna Künstlerhaus, he and Gustav Klimt became leading members of the Vienna Secession, which they helped to found in 1897. Here, he was able to present his designs to a group of cultured, forward-thinking, and well-off clients for the first time. In 1899, Hoffmann's reputation was already so established that he was appointed professor at the Kunstgewerbeschule in Vienna. At the start of 1900, there was a clear change of style in Hoffmann's work. With the renunciation of the swinging curves of the Secession and of Art Nouveau, he returned to classicist ideals and simple forms. The Scottish designers Charles Robert Ashbee and Charles Rennie Mackintosh were an important influence here. A period of intensive production now began in collaboration with the Jacob & Josef Kohn company, manufacturers of modern bentwood furniture. In 1908, a complete country house together with

interior decoration and furniture was constructed based on Hoffmann's designs. The construction of a villa complex at Hohe Warte in Vienna gave Hoffmann the opportunity to demonstrate his new form ideals. House and furnishings should be a unit, "... a house whose exterior [must] also reveal its interior."

With the establishment of the Vienna Werkstätte (1903–32), Hoffmann concentrated on his aim of overcoming the ornamental excesses of Art Nouveau and returning to simple design. The Sanatorium in Purkersdorf, near Vienna (1903–06), and the Palais Stoclet in Brussels demonstrate Hoffmann's innovative form intentions, both in their architecture and the interior decoration: strict formal detailing and simplicity of the cubic forms that continue through to the furnishings. All of Hoffmann's constructions from before the World War I show a timid, unconventional classicism and correspond to the upper middle class's need for representation.

From 1919 on, ill health forced Josef Hoffman to hand over management of his workshop for some time. However, he continued to create new designs and products until his death. After World War II, Hoffmann took on various official tasks, such as membership of the Arts Senate and the role of Austrian General Commissioner for the Biennale in Venice. The Wittmann furniture workshops began to reproduce Hoffmann furniture in the 1970s. Hoffmann's lamp designs have also been manufactured by hand by the Viennese company WOKA since the 1970s. *hd*

1870 Born on December 15 in Pirnitz, Moravia
FROM 1887 ON, attends the Höhere Staatsgewerbeschule in Brno
1892–95 Studies architecture at the Akademie der Bildenden Künste in Vienna; from 1894 on under Otto Wagner
1897 Founding member of the Vienna Secession
FROM 1899 ON, teaching post at the Vienna Kunstgewerbeschule (today Hochschule für Angewandte Kunst)
1900–02 Residences at Hohe Warte in Vienna
1903 Establishes the Vienna Werkstätte (with Fritz Wärndorfer and Koloman Moser)
1903 Purkersdorf Sanatorium near Vienna
1905–11 Palais Stoclet, Brussels
1914 Austrian Pavilion at the Werkbund Exhibition in Cologne
1924–25 Sonja Knips House, Vienna; Austrian Pavilion at the International Arts and Crafts Exhibition in Paris
1932 Terraced houses in the Vienna Werkbund settlement
1934 Austrian Pavilion for the Biennale in Venice
1956 Dies in Vienna on May 7

left page
Josef Hoffmann, Sitzmaschine armchair, 1908

above
Portrait of Josef Hoffmann

1833 The British Parliament passes the
Slavery Abolition Act

1857–1859 First world economic crisis

1887 First Sherlock Homes
novel is published

1848–1849 Revolutions in numerous
European countries

1871 Charles Darwin publishes
The Descent of Man

1895 Discovery of X-rays

1903–1904 British expedition
to Tibet

1830　1835　1840　1845　1850　1855　1860　1865　1870　1875　1880　1885　1890　1895　1900　1905　1910　1915

Eileen Gray, Adjustable Table E-1027,
side table, 1927

1919 Bauhaus founded by
Walter Gropius in Weimar

1946 First computer

1954–1962 Algerian War

1936 Charlie Chaplin, *Modern Times*

1960 The Beatles form

| 1920 | 1925 | 1930 | 1935 | 1940 | 1945 | 1950 | 1955 | 1960 | 1965 | 1970 | 1975 | 1980 | 1985 | 1990 | 1995 | 2000 | 2005 |

EILEEN GRAY

Eileen Gray started her career as a designer by designing exclusive lacquered furniture, but her breakthrough did not come until the age of 50 with the construction of her house E-1027 on the French Riviera and the accompanying innovative furniture. She consistently used functionality as an element to determine the design.

Original pieces by Gray today achieve top prices at auctions and reeditions of her most important designs are popular – and often copied – classics of modern design. However, the fact that Gray's name is spoken in the same breath as Le Corbusier, Breuer, and other icons of design history is a relatively new phenomenon. She was almost forgotten during her lifetime, and it was only from the 1970s on that her work was rediscovered.

While most artists of that time can be linked to a group or at least to a movement, Eileen Gray always remained independent. Although influences from the Dutch De Stijl group, Japonism, and Art Deco are indeed apparent, she did develop her own unique style as a lacquer artist, furniture designer, or later as an architect.

After studying painting in London, Gray, who was born in Ireland, moved to Paris in 1902. Here, she improved her knowledge of lacquer work, which she had acquired in London, and over a period of many years learned the subtleties of this art from the Japanese lacquer artist Seizo Sugawara. Gray made a name for herself with her designs for exclusive lacquer furniture and folding screens, and in 1922 she opened the Galerie Jean Désert. Whereas her work was initially very decorative and opulent, her style changed radically in the 1920s to a simpler design repertoire.

The formative influence in this development was – in addition to her contact with the artist group De Stijl and its austere geometric style and with the avant-garde "Union des Artistes Modernes" – the architect Jean Badovici. Gray also embraced modernity in her choice of materials, with steel tubing, aluminum, and glass replacing ivory, mother of pearl, and lacquer. The *Bibendum* chair (1929) and the *Adjustable Table E-1027* side table (1929) are examples of her modern, minimalist furniture, which was full of simple elegance as well as functionality. These classic pieces, still manufactured today as reeditions, were designs for her first house.

Badovici had encouraged the autodidact in her idea to design and decorate a house. In collaboration with Badovici she created the *E-1027* villa in Roquebrune on the French Riviera between 1926 and 1929. Gray created innovative integrated furniture for the L-shaped flat-roofed building and multipurpose single pieces of furniture from steel tubing, for example, the side table *E-1027*, which is still today considered a masterpiece of classic modern design and is probably Gray's most famous design. In addition to the functionality and the use of modern materials, her designs are also characterized by a charming lightness. The *Bibendum* chair thus references the eponymous Michelin tire man with its three sumptuous round cushions.

Although she took up the invitation from Le Corbusier to exhibit in his pavilion at the Paris Expo in 1937, at this time she was already leading a very reclusive life in the house she had designed, *Tempe à Pailla*, in the south of France. Gray's name then faded into obscurity until 1972, when furniture from the estate of the collector Jacques Doucet was auctioned off. *ch*

1878 Born near Enniscorthy in the county of Wexford, Ireland
1898–1902 Studies at the Slade School of Fine Art in London
1902 Moves to Paris
1919 Designs the interior of an apartment in the Rue de Lota in Paris
1922 Opens the Galerie Jean Désert
1926–29 Designs her first house, *E-1027*, in Roquebrune
1932–34 Designs her own house, *Tempe à Pailla*, in Castellar
1976 Dies in Paris

Portrait of Eileen Gray

WALTER GROPIUS

MARCEL BREUER

MARIANNE BRANDT

1849 Frédéric Chopin dies

1837 Louis Daguerre invents
daguerreotype

1853–1870 Haussmann's reno-
vation of Paris

1876 Invention of the telephone

1884 Robert Koch discovers
the cholera bacillus

1900 Sigmund Freud,
*The Interpretation
of Dreams*

1911 Wassily Kandinsky,
*Concerning the
Spiritual in Art*

1861 Abraham Lincoln sworn in as
president of the US

1914 Beginning of
World War I

1835 1840 1845 1850 1855 1860 1865 1870 1875 1880 1885 1890 1895 1900 1905 1910 1915 1920

Walter Gropius, F51 armchair,
Bauhaus Weimar, 1920, re-edition
by TECTA, Lauenförde

1937 Pablo Picasso, *Guernica*

1924 Thomas Mann, *Magic Mountain*

1946 UNESCO founded

| 1925 | 1930 | 1935 | 1940 | 1945 | 1950 | 1955 | 1960 | 1965 | 1970 | 1975 | 1980 | 1985 | 1990 | 1995 | 2000 | 2005 | 2010 |

WALTER GROPIUS

With Klee and Kandinsky as groomsmen and a honeymoon trip to Le Corbusier in Paris, Walter Gropius was part of the avant-garde movement of the interwar period. With his designs, which were always a synthesis of art and technique, the enthusiastic pioneer of modern art was a founder of "New Objectivity" in the industrial age.

Walter Gropius was primarily an architect. In accordance with his concept of "Unity in Art," he also designed furniture and other interior decoration objects such as textiles, wallpaper, lighting, and ceramics.

Initially, his pieces of furniture were very individual and influenced by craftsmanship as, together with Henry van de Velde of the German Werkbund artist organization, he fought against the standardization of design and for more creativity. For example, the furniture for the Fagus factory from 1911 has a strong personal signature; however, with regard to the construction, it was well suited to mass production. Gropius's Bauhaus office from 1923 is also symbolic of this phase: the austere lines of the lighting and the geometric shapes are broken up by bright carpets. The F51 executive chair, which he designed for this office, is today one of his best-known pieces of furniture with its unusual shape, the freestanding armrests, and the upholstery of leather and cavalry cloth.

The new technical opportunities in particular, and also the destruction of the world war periods caused Gropius to standardize his designs and constructions and to increase mass production. He devoted himself intensively to mass housing construction as a solution for town planning and social problems and also applied this train of thought to furniture. Rationalism, usefulness, and the shift toward modernity are therefore reflected in his later designs. The futuristic *TAC 1* tea service created for Rosenthal in 1969, which he designed for his office as part of his Studio Line, became very popular. In accordance with his concept of design, it should satisfy both material and spiritual requirements. With the extraordinary, tapered paunches and the hidden sliding lids, he created a tea service that is striking in its elegance. When he designed it, Gropius was already well into his 80s and he reflected on a successful career that had lasted for over five decades.

With the merger of the Kunstgewerbeschule and the Hochschule für bildende Künste in Weimar, Gropius wanted to create a completely new type of education with the Bauhaus school that was suited to modern industrial society. Here, artists, craftsmen, and architects could work together "on modern design," both in theory and in practice. The specially designed Bauhaus workshops were "basically laboratories for developing models ripe for mass production, implements typical of the present day [from the simplest household appliance to a complete dwelling] and continually improving them" (Gropius, 1925).

Gropius and his colleagues, including Ludwig Mies van der Rohe, Marcel Breuer, and Wilhelm Wagenfeld, developed many designs in this creative environment that are today considered modern classics and exhibited in design museums around the world. *nk*

1883 Born on May 18 in Berlin
1903–07 Studies at the technical universities in Munich and Berlin
1908–10 Works in the agency of Peter Behrens
1910 Gropius becomes a freelancer and a member of the German Werkbund artist association
1919 Appointment at the Kunstgewerbeschule and Hochschule für bildende Kunst in Weimar: merging and renaming of the two schools as the Staatliches Bauhaus
1934 Emigrates to England, director of the design department at Isokon
1937 Emigrates to the USA, professor of architecture at Harvard
1946 Founded the TAC agency (The Architects Collaborative)
1958 Highest Order of Merit with Star from the Federal Republic of Germany
1963 Honorary doctorate from the Freie Universität, Berlin
1969 Dies in Boston

Portrait of Walter Gropius, 1919

1848 French Revolution
(February Revolution)

1867 Karl Marx, *Das Kapital*

1887–1889 Eiffel Tower
built in Paris

1879 Albert Einstein is born

1909–1910 Henri
Matisse, *La Danse*

1911 Wassily Kandinsky,
Impression III

1903 First powered flight by the Wright brothers

1835　1840　1845　1850　1855　1860　1865　1870　1875　1880　1885　1890　1895　1900　1905　1910　1915　1920

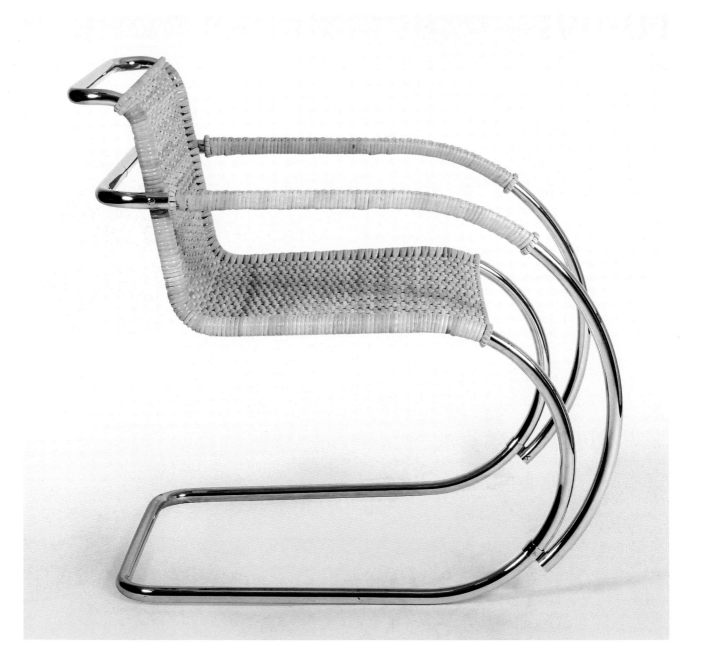

Ludwig Mies van der Rohe, D24 chair,
1927, re-edition by TECTA, Lauenförde

1925/26 Walter Gropius,
Bauhaus, Dessau

1939–1945 World War II

1949 Founding of the Federal
Republic of Germany

1925 1930 1935 1940 1945 1950 1955 1960 1965 1970 1975 1980 1985 1990 1995 2000 2005 2010

LUDWIG MIES VAN DER ROHE

Designs by Ludwig Mies van der Rohe made a point of reducing everything to the bare minimum. As a result, they have become both modern precursors as well as timeless classics.

As a leading representative of the International Style, Ludwig Mies van der Rohe dedicated himself to modernity in both his architecture and his furniture designs, and he experimented with the latest technologies. His target group was the modern city dweller and, in contrast to many of his contemporaries, he was less concerned with mass production and social housing construction, focusing instead more on technology-based design combined with quality and elegance. True to his principle of "less is more," he created modern design classics with the *Barcelona* chair and the *Brno* chair, which still enjoy cult status today.

After training as a stonemason and bricklayer in Aachen, the young Ludwig Mies moved to Berlin, where he studied architecture. He gained his first work experience with Bruno Paul and in the agency of Peter Behrens, where he also got to know Walter Gropius and Le Corbusier. When he opened his own office in 1912, he extended his surname with the maiden name of his mother and from then on achieved increasing recognition. Mies van der Rohe first received public attention when he introduced the revolutionary "skin and bones" architecture with the construction of the glass skyscraper on Friedrichstrasse near the Berlin railway station. From then on, he worked on many important projects, such as the Stuttgart Weissenhof estate, the German Pavilion at the Expo in Barcelona, and the *Villa Tugendhat*, designing both the houses as well as the matching furniture. In 1930, he became director of the Bauhaus in Dessau until it was closed in 1933.

The most famous furniture designs by Ludwig Mies van der Rohe were created in collaboration with the interior designer Lilly Reich. Both viewed the tubular steel cantilever chair as the epitome of modernity and were fascinated by the design opportunities offered by tubular steel. With the *MR 10* and the *MR 20*, which were constructed from a bent, semicircular steel tube and a wickerwork seat,

they created both the most elegant cantilever chair yet and also the first chair to actually allow the user to swing. The subsequent *MR 50* and *MR 90* designs can be seen as a further development in tubular steel cantilever chairs in that they used flat steel and steel tape. The new material had a much more refined appearance but was also significantly more expensive to produce as it had to be worked by hand.

Mies van der Rohe and Reich's most famous furniture design was probably the *MR 90*, which was created in 1929 when he was commissioned to construct the German Pavilion at the Exposición Internacional de Barcelona, and they designed the interior together. Inspired by *sella curulis*, the Roman curule seat, they created a chair with an X-shaped frame of bent, chromium-plated flat steel, strung with leather straps, on which lay leather cushions. Thanks to the materials used – steel and leather – the stool had both a luxurious and modern appearance and was thus a stylish and yet modern throne for King Alfonso XIII of Spain, who held the opening ceremony in the German Pavilion. *nk*

1886 Born on March 27 in Aachen
1900 Trains as a stonemason and bricklayer in Aachen
1905 Moves to Berlin, studies at the Kunstgewerbeschule Berlin, works for the furniture designer Bruno Paul
1908–11 Architecture agency of Peter Behrens
1912 Opens his own office in Berlin
1926 Director of the Werkbund exhibition Die Wohnung (designs tubular steel furniture)
1928 Patents the suspension system in the MR10 and MR20 cantilever chairs and Lilly Reich's natural wickerwork as a collaborative design
1929 German Pavilion at the Expo Barcelona
1930 Haus Tugendhat in Brno
1930–33 Director of the Bauhaus in Dessau
1937 Emigrates to Chicago
FROM 1938 ON, sets up own architecture agency and is professor at the Illinois Institute of Technology
1969 Dies in Chicago

Portrait of Mies van der Rohe

1848 French Revolution (February Revolution)

1857 Gustave Flaubert, *Madame Bovary*

1870/71 Franco-Prussian War

1888 Vincent van Gogh, *Sunflowers*

1900 French Métro is opened

1914 Marcel Duchamp's first readymade, *Bottle Rack*

1835 1840 1845 1850 1855 1860 1865 1870 1875 1880 1885 1890 1895 1900 1905 1910 1915 1920

Le Corbusier, Pierre Jeanneret, and Charlotte Perriand, LC4 chaise longue, 1928

1927 Charles Lindbergh flies nonstop
from New York to Paris

1958 Yves Klein opens the exhibition
Le Vide in Paris

1940–1944 German occupation of France

1962–1968 Ludwig Mies van der Rohe,
Neue Nationalgalerie, Berlin

1925   1930   1935   1940   1945   1950   1955   1960   1965   1970   1975   1980   1985   1990   1995   2000   2005   2010

LE CORBUSIER

As a mastermind of the urban lifestyle, Le Corbusier was convinced that good design would lead to improved living standards, and he became one of the most influential personalities of design, architecture, and urban planning in the 20th century.

Modern design and modern architecture are synonymous with the name Le Corbusier. It was during study tours from 1907 to 1911 and whilst working in well-known architecture agencies in Vienna, Berlin, and Paris that the young Charles-Édouard Jeanneret-Gris acquired the basic knowledge that would subsequently make him one of the most renowned architects, urban planners, and designers, As early as 1914, he succeeded in designing a skeletal system in reinforced concrete that made it possible to build multistory constructions with ready-made individual concrete parts. In 1917, he settled in Paris. As it was not yet the right time for his architectural ideas, he devoted himself to painting and published the journal *L'Esprit Nouveau*. From 1920 on, he presented his avant-garde architectural concepts in this journal and used the pseudonym Le Corbusier for the first time, which he chose in memory of his grandfather (Lecorbésier).

Although Le Corbusier's works extended over five decades, he designed furniture mainly in the late 1920s and early 1930s and always in collaboration with his cousin Pierre Jeanneret and the architect Charlotte Perriand. These furniture designs conformed with his functional architectural principles and were intended to correspond to modern living conditions.

In 1925, he designed a pavilion for the *Exposition Internationale des Arts Décoratifs* with his cousin Pierre, which contained paintings as well as the first furniture designs by the two men. After employing the architect Charlotte Perriand at his agency, the team of three began to experiment with pieces of furniture. Inspired by the designs of their colleagues Marcel Breuer, Mart Stam, and Mies van der Rohe and by the design opportunities offered by industrially manufactured steel, the first models of the *LC* series were created and exhibited for the first time at the Salon d'Automne in Paris in 1929. They are a true manifestation of modern furniture design and

are limited to just a few basic shapes to accommodate human needs.

The *LC4* couch and his famous quote "A house is a machine for living in, a chair is a machine for sitting in" clarify the principles of Le Corbusier design. Like machines, furniture should fulfill functional requirements and, consequently, make this evident in their design. The structure of the *LC4*, or "relaxation machine," is kept as simple as possible, and is clearly and perfectly modified to human ergonomics. The S-shaped sleeping area is reminiscent of a resting person and is itself an invitation to relax. Like all furniture designs by Corbusier, the couch also plays with contrasts, for example organic on inorganic material, hard on soft surfaces, and angular on curving forms. The interesting point about this couch is that as a piece of furniture, the recliner can also be seen as a symbol for modern man. Now that new, urban lifestyle habits have less and less to do with physical work, they allow for more leisure time and relaxation. In 1964, the Italian furniture manufacturer Cassina purchased the exclusive rights to Le Corbusier's furniture designs and is still the only authorized manufacturer of his furniture designs. *nk*

1887 Born as Charles-Édouard Jeanneret-Gris in La Chaux-de-Fonds, Switzerland
1900–07 Studies painting and architecture at the Kunstgewerbeschule in La Chaux-de-Fonds
1907–11 Study tours with appointments in leading European architecture agencies (Vienna, Berlin, Paris)
1912–14 Teacher at the Kunstgewerbeschule in La Chaux-de-Fonds
1917 Moves to Paris
1919 Publishes the journal *L'Esprit Nouveau*, uses the pseudonym for the first time
1927 Designs for the Weissenhofsiedlung in Stuttgart
1928 Founder member of the Congrès Internationaux d'Architecture Moderne (CIAM)
1929 Exhibits the first furniture range at the Salon d'Automne, Paris
1930 Marries Yvonne Gallis; French citizenship
1933 The CIAM publishes the urban planning manifesto *Athens Charter*
1965 Dies in Roquebrune-Cap-Martin, France

Portrait of Le Corbusier

GEORGE CARWARDINE

WALTER GROPIUS

WILHELM WAGENFELD

1886 Statue of Liberty erected in
New York Harbor

1865 Slavery abolished in the U.S.

1851 First World's Fair in London

1874 First Impressionist exhibition
in Paris

1895 First Venice Biennale

1900 Boxer Rebellion in China

1835 1840 1845 1850 1855 1860 1865 1870 1875 1880 1885 1890 1895 1900 1905 1910 1915 1920

914 Assassination of Archduke Franz Ferdinand
of Austria on June 28; World War I breaks out

1929 Stock market crash heralds
global economic crisis

1939–1945 World War II

1942 Edward Hopper, *Nighthawks*

1948 Declaration of Independence of
the State of Israel, May 14

| 1925 | 1930 | 1935 | 1940 | 1945 | 1950 | 1955 | 1960 | 1965 | 1970 | 1975 | 1980 | 1985 | 1990 | 1995 | 2000 | 2005 | 2010 |

GEORGE CARWARDINE

Many important and popular everyday objects are by-products of a much more fundamental development, and truly great designs often emerge from the solution to a specific need.

The Briton George Carwardine, born in 1887, was employed in the late 1920s as a freelance engineer in the automobile industry in Bath, where he developed and constructed springs and wheel suspensions. One of his most important ideas was a suspension system developed in 1932, which could be placed in any position and which would not move. Two springs were connected via a rod in such a way that the traction was balanced and the arm connected to the rod kept its position. The mechanism was intended for use in the automobile industry but implementation was too expensive and its purpose was unclear.

However, Carwardine soon realized that the principle could be applied to other areas. With the original idea of creating focused light for his own workplace, he created an adjustable work lamp in his workshops that consisted of one foot, a swivelling and folding arm balanced on four springs, and a lampshade to protect against glare and burning. The lamp was very effective and, after Carwadine had made some improvements, he patented his design the same year. The *Anglepoise*, as he called his lamp, was born.

At first he produced some of the lamps himself and sold them under the name of his own company, Cardine Accessories, but demand for his practical work lamp grew quickly and in 1934, Carwardine initially licensed the design for production by the Terry Spring Company, which supplied his springs. They advertised the lamp as "precise" and "energy-saving" and marketed it very successfully to doctors, dentists, and workshops under the name *Type 1208*. Carwadine could now devote his time to the further development of the suspension system and in 1936, he brought out the more elegant *Type 1227*, an Art Deco variant with three springs for use at home. Sales figures for the 1227 quickly overtook the 1208, and when Jacob Jacobsen purchased the rights for the lamp for the European and American markets in 1937, it finally became a bestseller. Jacobsen

modified the design and from 1938 on sold it as *Luxo L-1*. The inventor of the *Anglepoise* died in 1948 but his ideas live on: the animation studio Pixar commemorated the *Luxo L1* variant with a short film, *Luxo Jr*, and this established the studio's own success in the animation of objects that is now characteristic of its cartoon films. Even so, the Terry Spring Company had to file for bankruptcy in 2001 as the license used by Jacobsen to sell *Luxo L1* restricted it to the British market and the company could no longer compete with cheaper competitors from Asia. *jr*

1887 George Carwardine was born on April 4 in Bath, England
1901–05 Engineer apprenticeship at the Whiting Auto Works
1916 Works manager and chief designer at the Horstman Car Company
1924 Establishes the Cardine Accessories engineering company in Bath
1929 Cardine Accessories is closed temporarily and he returns to Horstman
1931 Works as a freelance engineer and inventor of suspensions
1932 Patents the *Anglepoise* mechanism
1934 The Terry Spring Company manufactures the first *Anglepoise* lamp (Type 1208)
1936 The *Type 1227* is launched on the market
1937 Grants the production rights to the Norwegian engineer Jacob Jacobsen, who sells the lamps under the name *Luxo L1*
1947 *Anglepoise* is protected as a brand name
1948 Carwardine dies at the age of 60
1986 *Luxo L1* is the subject of the animated short film *Luxo Jr*

left page
George Carwardine, Anglepoise lamp, 1932

PIET MONDRIAN

WASSILY KANDINSKY

1861–1865 American Civil War

1848 Start of the California Gold Rush

1883–1885 First skyscrapers
in Chicago

1907 Pablo Picasso, *Les Demoiselles d'Avignon*

1892 Premiere of Tchaikovsky's ballet
The Nutcracker in St. Petersburg

1914–1918 World War I

1840   1845   1850   1855   1860   1865   1870   1875   1880   1885   1890   1895   1900   1905   1910   1915   1920   1925

1950 Josef Albers, *Homage to the Square*

1924 André Breton,
Surrealist Manifesto

1942 Peggy Guggenheim opens the gallery
"Art of This Century" in New York

1936–1939 Spanish Civil War

| 1930 | 1935 | 1940 | 1945 | 1950 | 1955 | 1960 | 1965 | 1970 | 1975 | 1980 | 1985 | 1990 | 1995 | 2000 | 2005 | 2010 | 2015 |

GERRIT RIETVELD

The Utrecht designer and architect Gerrit Rietveld was an expert on the Der Stijl movement who carried out pioneering work in architecture and furniture design.

The Dutch architect and designer is best known for his chair designs. Gerrit Rietveld rose from being a master carpenter to become one of the most important artists of the De Stijl group. He gained influence first and foremost with the *Rietveld-Schröder House* in Utrecht (1924) and the *Red and Blue Chair* (1918). The main features of his work, which was influenced by De Stijl, are the strict geometry and the reduction of the color palette to the primary colors of red, blue, and yellow.

Born in 1888, Gerrit Rietveld initially trained as a carpenter in his father's business. He acquired his architectural knowledge at evening classes held by the architect P. J. C Klaarhamer, whose architectural company was able to offer Rietveld solid financial backing through frequent commissions, thus providing him with the chance to engage intensively with the new design opportunities. Klaarhamer also acquainted Rietveld with the ideas of the new De Stijl movement. Rietveld soon joined this group, whose members included Piet Mondrian, Theo van Doesburg, Robert van't Hoff, and other renowned painters and architects. Their objective was the universal renewal of the arts through purely objective, geometric, and color-reduced design, which – in addition to painting and sculpture – should be applied to all everyday objects.

Around 1917, Rietveld, who in the meantime had established his own furniture workshop, received a commission to create furniture, based on the designs of Frank Lloyd Wright, for the Verloop House built by Robert van't Hoff in Huis ter Heide. These initial furniture designs show his familiarity with the De Stijl concepts of form from early on. Between 1917 and 1918, Rietveld designed his famous *Red and Blue Chair*. However, it was not until 1923 that the chair was given its final form with characteristic bright paint in the primary colors. With this piece of furniture, which seemed like a manifestation of De Stijl philosophy, Rietveld had created a completely new furniture prototype:

in its most familiar variant, the chair has a total height of 88 cm and is created from one board cut into 13 pieces of square timber, two slats for the armrests, and two slats for the seat and back, making it suitable for industrial production. The technique used to join the various pieces was also innovative: the individual wooden parts are no longer mortised but held together with dowels instead. The colors applied later are from the specific palette of primary colors used by De Stijl.

They are, however, more than mere decoration, for they also comply with the structural conditions. All parts of the frame for the square timber are black, their cut areas yellow. The seat has a stripe of intense blue, while the supporting and load-resisting backrest is aggressive red. The chair, like no other object, combines elements from both the formal and the functional De Stijl ideals. It is both a work of art and a utility object, and demonstrates the utopian vision of another ideal form of the environment, interpreted in the same way by Rietveld in the *Rietveld-Schröder House* – where visible integrated steel joists include the structural elements in the design, sliding walls structure the upper floor, and unsupported corner windows open the rooms to the outside.

In subsequent years, Rietveld switched his main activity to the design and decoration of interior rooms and complete residences. In 1930/31, he developed standard construction elements for the City of Utrecht that could be arranged in different ways as finished parts and connected as residential units. Rietveld was also experimental and innovative in furniture design. This led to the creation in 1932 to 1934 of the *Zig-Zag Chair*, which joined four boards in a classic right angle in the backrest and at a bold 45 degrees at the base and thus managed without the standard four chair legs.

As a founding member of the International Congress for Modern Architecture, 1928, Rietveld campaigned for modern design until his death. *hd*

1888 Born on July 24 in Utrecht
1900 Apprenticeship in his father's furniture workshop
1906 Evening classes with the Utrecht architect P. J. C. Klaarhamer
1917 Establishes his own furniture workshop in Utrecht
1918 *Red and Blue Chair*, final version 1923/24
1919–31 Member of the De Stijl group
1924 Rietveld-Schröder House
1932 Terraced house for four families at the Werkbund Exhibition in Vienna
FROM 1946 employed mainly as an architect, also continues with designs for furniture and interior decoration
1954 Dutch Pavilion for the Biennale in Venice
1963–72 Van Gogh Museum Amsterdam (completed by the employees van Tricht and van Dillen)
1964 Dies on June 25 in the Rietveld-Schröder House

left page
Gerrit Rietveld, Red Blue Chair, 1917–23

above
Portrait of Gerrit Rietveld

1883 Opening of the Metropolitan
Opera in New York

1902 Alfred Stieglitz's *Camera Work*
is founded

1853–1856 Crimean War

1873 Claude Monet,
Impression, Sunrise

1896 First modern Olympic
Games

1911 Ernest Rutherford develops
his model of the atom

1840 1845 1850 1855 1860 1865 1870 1875 1880 1885 1890 1895 1900 1905 1910 1915 1920 1925

Gio Ponti, Superleggera chair, 1957

1955 *The Family of Man* exhibition
at MoMA in New York

925 Invention of television

1962 Cuban Missile Crisis

1940 McDonald's is founded

1970 British rock band Queen form

1930 1935 1940 1945 1950 1955 1960 1965 1970 1975 1980 1985 1990 1995 2000 2005 2010 2015

GIO PONTI

Gio Ponti is often called the father of Italian design because his publications as well as his own designs had a great influence on Italy's understanding of art.

With buildings in 13 countries, 1,000 architectural sketches, 25 years as a teacher, articles in 560 journals (which he also published himself), and designs for 120 different companies, Gio Ponti was not only extremely productive throughout his career but also highly versatile. He was an architect, craftsman, editor, writer, set designer, and industrial designer. In his designs, he always aimed to be modern without forgetting the old ways, and the combination of modern and tradition thus became Ponti's trademark.

In the 1920s, Ponti, along with Emilio Lancia, Giovanni Muzio, and Tommaso Buzzi, was one of the most important proponents of the Novecento style, which was inspired by Art Deco as well as by the Vienna Werkstätte and classicism. He created handcrafted vases and porcelain and designed furniture for the La Rinascente department store. As the artistic director for the ceramics manufacturer Richard Ginori, Ponti was able to give new impulse to the art of industrial design by decorating simple shapes with neoclassical designs. In the late 1920s and 1930s, he again devoted himself to architecture and turned to rationalism, albeit in a rather reserved way. With his Milan *Domus* houses in particular, which from the outside looked like typical Milan townhouses, but inside were highly innovative with flexible rooms and modular furniture, Ponti showed his talent for unifying old and new. He created an Italian design classic in 1947 with the *La Cornuta* coffee machine, with its chrome, streamlined, and technically elegant silhouette.

Another of Ponti's masterpieces is the *Superleggera* chair, which he created in the 1950s. After a ten-year thought process, he managed to develop this period furniture with the manufacturer Cassina. The chair combines a fragile appearance with an indestructible stability and was ideal for the cramped apartments of the 1950s. To prove its stability, Ponti once threw it out of a fourth-floor window – the chair remained intact. Inspired by the traditional *Chiavari* chairs, with *Superleggera* Ponti opted for a new arrangement of the cross braces and, by using ash, he was able reduce the radius of the chair legs, which made the chair more delicate but also more stable. Although he remained true to the traditional caned seat, he chose black paint for the wood. He thus created a chair that was striking in its Italian tradition, classical elegance, and modern shape yet still represented the weakened rationalism that was so typical for Ponti. At the start of the 1960s, the mass-produced *Superleggera* became a symbol of the economic miracle in Italy and established Cassina's route to becoming an ambitious design company.

In addition to his original designs, Ponti was also influential on other levels. His journal *Domus*, which he himself published from 1928 on, became the most influential magazine for design and architecture. As a founder of the Milan Trienniale, he always supported the work of progressive designers, and during his career as a professor, which lasted for almost 30 years, he also influenced subsequent generations of designers. *nk*

1891 Born on October 18 in Milan
UNTIL 1921 Studies architecture in Milan
1921–22 Architecture office of Emilio Lancia and Mino Fiocchi
1923 Artistic director at the ceramics manufacturer Richard Ginori
1926–33 Architecture agency with Emilio Lancia
1925–79 Director of the Biennale in Monza
1928 Establishes the journal *Domus*
1933 Manager at Fontana Arte
1936–61 Professor at Politecnico di Milano
1941 Establishes the journal *Stile*
1948 *La Cornuta* coffee machine for La Pavoni
1953 *Serie P* sanitary ware for Ideal Standard, *Distex* chair for Cassina
1957 *Superleggera* chair for Cassina
1979 Dies on September 16 in Milan

Portrait of Gio Ponti

MARIANNE BRANDT

PAUL KLEE

LUDWIG MIES VAN DER ROHE

1905 German Expressionist group
Die Brücke is founded in
Dresden

1929 The Museum
of Modern Art
opens in New
York

1888 Vincent van Gogh, *The Night Café*

1916 Albert Einstein, *Theory of Relativity*

1845　1850　1855　1860　1865　1870　1875　1880　1885　1890　1895　1900　1905　1910　1915　1920　1925　1930

Marianne Brandt, MT 49 tea infuser, 1924

1945 Atom bombs dropped on
Hiroshima and Nagasaki

1961 Founding of Amnesty
International

1989 Fall of the Berlin Wall

1933 Adolf Hitler comes to power

1949 Founding of the German
Democratic Republic

1971 First Starbucks opens

1955 Beginning of Pop Art

1935 1940 1945 1950 1955 1960 1965 1970 1975 1980 1985 1990 1995 2000 2005 2010 2015 2020

MARIANNE BRANDT

She never achieved the fame of her male colleagues, but as one of the few women in the Bauhaus movement, Marianne Brandt made her name with beautiful yet functional metalwork. Some of her most famous designs — for coffee and tea services and ashtrays, for example — were created while she was still a student, and some are still manufactured to the same design today.

Weaving, bookbinding, pottery – these were the classic fields of the Bauhaus movement in which women were strongly represented. However, Marianne Brandt was one of the few Bauhaus women to assert herself in a male domain: the metal workshop. When Walter Gropius opened the Staatliche Bauhaus in Weimar in 1919, he spoke out in favor of absolute equality, but it soon became apparent that reality was quite different and the female students were forced out of many workshops.

Brandt, who arrived at the Bauhaus school in 1923, completed her apprenticeship in the metal workshop, which was directed at this time by the Hungarian constructivist László Moholy-Nagy. Impressed by the work of the new student, he encouraged her to specialize in this area. She soon made a name for herself with timeless and beautiful pieces of metalwork – with innovative and functional cutlery, in particular. Later, Brandt even became the deputy manager of the metal workshop and was thus one of the few women at the Bauhaus school to hold a managerial role.

As early as 1924 and while still a student, Marianne Brandt created a real masterpiece with the design of a tea and coffee service. This lavishly worked service in brass and ebony was in the Art Deco style and is striking with its contrast of materials and the clear, bold combination of geometric shapes. The combination of spheres, hemispheres, and cylinder shapes, as well as the asymmetrically arranged handles, are echoes of Russian constructivism and the Dutch De Stijl movement. In 1985, this service, originally manufactured as individual pieces, was reissued by the Alessi company.

"Art and technology, a new unit!" Gropius's demand was put on the program after the Bauhaus school moved to Dessau in 1925. Cooperation with industry was promoted and mass production became more professional. Elegant utility products were to be made accessible to a wider public. Brandt succeeded in implementing the Bauhaus philosophy of industrial product design in an exemplary manner. Over the next few years, she designed a series of utility objects, including metal ashtrays, jugs, and bowls. From 1927 on, she turned to the design of electric lamps. One of the most famous designs from those years is the bedside lamp *Kandem*, which she designed in 1928 together with Hin Bredendieck. The lamp, which is painted in black or white and has a movable arm, is a prime example of functional, simple, and modern design.

After leaving the Bauhaus school at the end of the 1920s, Brandt worked at Walter Gropius's Berlin architecture agency, where she initially designed interior furnishings before working for three years as head of design at the Ruppelwerke metal goods factory. After the war, she taught at the Hochschule für Bildende Künste in Dresden and later at the Institut für industrielle Gestaltung in Berlin. However, she was unable to recreate her early success as a designer and devoted herself more and more to painting and sculpture until her later years. *ch*

1893 Born Marianne Liebe in Chemnitz
1911–18 Studies painting at the Grand Ducal-Saxon Hochschule für Bildende Kunst in Weimar
1919 Marries the Norwegian painter Erik Brandt
1923 Attends the introductory course at the Bauhaus School in Weimar, then studies texture and materials under Josef Albers and László Moholy-Nagy and artistic composition under Paul Klee and Wassily Kandinsky
1925–28 Apprentice, then employee and deputy manager of the metal workshop at the Bauhaus school
1929 Works in Walter Gropius's construction agency in Berlin
1930–33 Manager of the design department at the Ruppelwerke metal goods factory in Gotha
1933–49 Freelance artist and applied artist
1949–54 Lecturer in wood, metal, and ceramics at the Hochschule für Werkkunst in Dresden and at the Institut für industrielle Gestaltung in Berlin-Weissensee
1955 Moves to Chemnitz
1983 Dies in Kirchberg, Saxony

Portrait of Marianne Brandt

1866 Civil Rights Act extending
the rights of emancipated
slaves

1884 Mark Twain publishes the
Adventures of Huckleberry Finn

1912 Sinking of the *Titanic*

1901 Theodore Roosevelt sworn
in as president of the US

1928 Andy
Warhol
is born

| 1845 | 1850 | 1855 | 1860 | 1865 | 1870 | 1875 | 1880 | 1885 | 1890 | 1895 | 1900 | 1905 | 1910 | 1915 | 1920 | 1925 | 1930 |

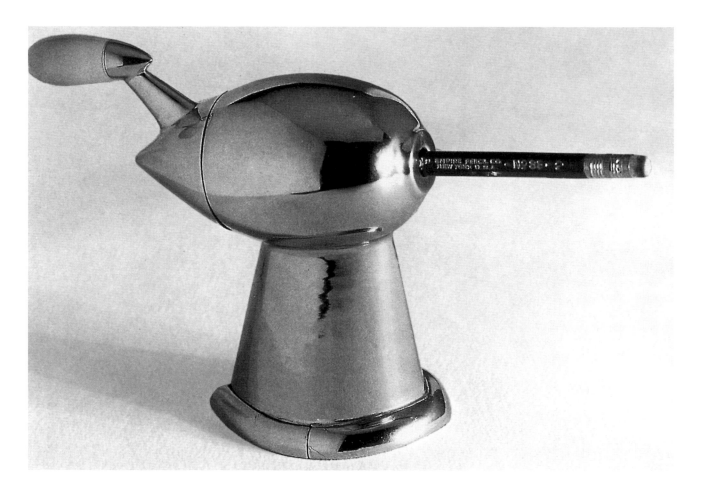

Raymond Loewy, pencil sharpener, 1933

1941 Pearl Harbor attack

1955–1968 Civil rights movement
in the U.S.

1982 Production of the first commercial
cd-player

1963 Roy Lichtenstein, *Whaam!*

1949 Mao Zedong founds the
People's Republic of China

1991 World Wide Web (WWW) cleared
for general use

1973 Watergate scandal

1935   1940   1945   1950   1955   1960   1965   1970   1975   1980   1985   1990   1995   2000   2005   2010   2015   2020

RAYMOND LOEWY

For more than 50 years, Raymond Loewy influenced the tastes of the Western world like no other. "I can claim," stated the industrial designer retrospectively and rather immodestly, "to have made the daily life of the 20th century more beautiful."

In 1919, the Frenchman emigrated to the US, where he first worked as a window dresser for New York department stores and as a fashion designer for *Vogue, Harper's Bazaar,* and *Vanity Fair.* His career change came ten years later when the British office furniture manufacturer Gestetner commissioned him to create a new design for one of their copying machines within a few days. Loewy used plasticine to create the prototype of a new elegant cover for the machine, which subsequently became a best seller. He had thus discovered a completely new approach, which he continued to use for a number of diverse industrial mass products: whether it was a kitchen appliance or an automobile, most of the less attractive mechanical parts were hidden beneath an elegant, modern exterior. Today, product design is a matter of course, but in the 1930s, this was a radical new way of thinking. For Loewy, the potential of his ideas was apparent immediately: "Between two products equal in price, function, and quality, the one with the most attractive exterior will win."

In 1934, Loewy made a breakthrough with a new design for the *Coldspot* refrigerator for Sears Roebuck, the first domestic appliance to advertise its aesthetic design and become a sensational success. Loewy's idea of beauty was the streamlined shape. The rounded edges, the extended, flowing shapes, and also the cover of gleaming chrome suggested speed, and these elements can also be seen in his aerodynamic designs for the steam locomotives for the Pennsylvania Railroad Company, as well as in the Studebaker automobiles, for example in the *Starliner* coupé with its curving fenders (1953) and in the *Scenicruiser* bus for Greyhound (1954).

Based on vehicle design, whereby the optimum air stream enables greater speed, the "Streamline Design" symbolized the new mobility and vitality of American society and was applied to a variety of products. Even Loewy's famous, albeit never manufactured prototype for a pencil sharpener in 1933 pays homage to streamlined design.

From the toothpaste tube to the ocean steamer, from porcelain tableware to the porthole for the NASA Skylab, there was almost nothing that Loewy did not want to redesign. He designed logos and packaging for such industrial giants as Coca-Cola, Lucky Strike, Exxon, and Shell. In the end, thanks to intensive self-promotion, the all-around designer became a star and was written about with admiration in a cover story in *Time* magazine in 1949: "He streamlines the sales curve." In fact Loewy did not stop at product design. With his large employee base and offices in New York, Chicago, London, and Paris, what he offered the customer was the complete package instead, which, in addition to product design, also included a concept for optimization of marketing, packaging, and sales. Thus he succeeded in the aestheticization and commercialization of private consumption. He reduced his design philosophy to the acronym MAYA – "Most Advanced, Yet Acceptable." *ch*

1893 Born in Paris
1910–19 Studies at the Université de Paris and the École de Lanneau, graduates as an engineer
1919 Emigrates to the US
1919–29 Window dresser and illustrator in New York
1929 Opens a design agency in New York; redesigns the Gestetner copying machine
1933 Prototype of a streamlined pencil sharpener
1934 Redesigns the *Coldspot* refrigerator for Sears Roebuck; *Hupmobile* car for the Hupp Motor Company
1938 *President* car for Studebaker
1940 *Silversides* bus for Greyhound
1951 Publishes the autobiography *Never Leave Well Enough Alone*
1953 *Starliner* car for Studebaker; opens a Paris office
1954 *Scenicruiser* bus for Greyhound; *Form 2000* porcelain tableware for Rosenthal
1967 Start of cooperation with NASA
1986 Dies in Monte Carlo

Portrait of Raymond Loewy

POUL HENNINGSEN

NAUM GABO

MARCEL DUCHAMP

1877 Leo Tolstoy publishes *Anna Karenina*

1903 Henry Ford establishes the
Ford Motor Company in Detroit

1867 The Alaska Purchase by the
United States

1888 First crossing of the Greenland
ice cap by Fridtjof Nansen

1919–1933 Prohibition
in the US

1845	1850	1855	1860	1865	1870	1875	1880	1885	1890	1895	1900	1905	1910	1915	1920	1925	1930

1931 Completion of the Empire State Building by William van Alen

1955 First documenta exhibition in Kassel, Germany

1983 Production of the first commercial mobile phone

1961 Construction of the Berlin Wall

1948 UN Declaration of Human Rights

1971 Founding of Greenpeace

1935 1940 1945 1950 1955 1960 1965 1970 1975 1980 1985 1990 1995 2000 2005 2010 2015 2020

POUL HENNINGSEN

Often referred to by the Danes as just PH, Poul Henningsen, architect, author, critic, and designer, was one of the central figures of cultural life in Denmark between the two world wars.

Today, the name Poul Henningsen can almost be used as a synonym for "Danish lighting design." However, it was initially his written works that received most attention after he abandoned his studies. As a journalist and art critic, Henningsen always strove to link culture to politics and he created the slogan: "All political art is bad – all good art is political." In his most famous work, *What about Culture?* from 1933, he criticized cultural life in Denmark, which at the time was characterized by an elitist and antimodern attitude. He also took part in public discussions during the postwar period and fought against the artistic arrogance of Scandinavian design.

As a designer and with his revolutionary lights, Henningsen was one of the most important representatives of Danish functionalism. In his designs, the focus was on the quality of light. He himself grew up with the gentle light of the petroleum lamp and it was his declared objective not to "flood the home with light" but instead to make it a snug and relaxing place. His designs were based on scientific investigations into the size, shape, material, and position of lampshades and used the refraction of light to create soft, glare-free lighting. He used slats as diffusers to refract the light and to provide the precisely calculated diffusion with their brightly painted undersides. In addition, the combination of reflectors in different sizes united both direct and indirect illumination. His light designs could create lighting that did not glare and that let the difference between the lit and unlit space become fluid. His first design was the three-shaded *PH lamp* made of brass and opal glass (1924). It was exhibited in the Danish Pavilion at the *Exposition des Arts Decoratifs* in Paris. Other international design and architecture colleagues integrated it into their room designs, including Ludwig Mies van der Rohe, who used it in the living area of the Villa Tugendhat (see page 29). This development also won the *PH lamps* great recognition outside Scandinavia. Until his death,

Poul Henningsen created more than 100 lighting designs for the *PH* series, which were all based on his original idea of using shades and diffusers to create a warm, diffused light. The best-known include the *PH Septima* (1927), whereby four additional diffusers of frosted glass were added to the three original lampshades, the *PH Louvre* with 13 concentrically arranged metal shades that diffuse the light to all sides, and the *PH Kogelen* (1957), also known as *Artichoke*, in which the lightbulb is surrounded by scale-like copper plates that resemble the heart of an artichoke.

Even though his lights were initially used mainly in offices and public institutions, with their modern design, combination of soft light, and their perfect light function, they quickly became popular dining-room lights and modern design classics. *nk*

1894 Born on September 4 in Ordrup
1908–10 Studies painting at the TU Copenhagen
1911–14 Studies architecture at the Polytechnic Institute of Copenhagen
1917–21 Art critic for the *Klingen* newspaper
FROM 1924 Designs lights and furniture
FROM 1926 Production of *PH* lamps at Louis Poulsen
1933–45 Scriptwriter and journalist
1943–45 Flees to Sweden
1958 *Kogelen (Artichoke)* lamp
1967 Dies in Hillerød

left page
Poul Henningsen, PH Kogelen, Artichoke lamp, 1958, re-edition by Louis Poulsen, 2008

above
Portrait of Poul Henningsen

1883 Friedrich Nietzsche publishes *Thus Spoke Zarathustra*

1897 Tate Gallery is founded in London

1919 Founding of the Weimar Republic

| 1850 | 1855 | 1860 | 1865 | 1870 | 1875 | 1880 | 1885 | 1890 | 1895 | 1900 | 1905 | 1910 | 1915 | 1920 | 1925 | 1930 | 1935 |

Alvar Aalto, cantilever chair No. 31 (now No. 42), re-edition by ARTEK

| 1940 | 1945 | 1950 | 1955 | 1960 | 1965 | 1970 | 1975 | 1980 | 1985 | 1990 | 1995 | 2000 | 2005 | 2010 | 2015 | 2020 | 2025 |

ALVAR AALTO

Alvar Aalto was a central figure in international modern design. With his innovative pieces of furniture, including the Aalto vase, he succeeded in connecting the naturalism of Finnish romanticism with modern ideals in a playful manner.

Anyone waiting for a delayed Finnair aeroplane in the 1950s could possibly blame Alvar Aalto for this. For even at that time, the Finn was part of the architect and designer elite and thus one of the few people for whom scheduled flights would wait.

At just 25 years of age, Aalto opened his own architecture agency and even at that time considered himself a star: he placed his name at the entrance in two-foot-high letters. A short time later, this proved to be justified, for even after his first projects, influential critics ranked him alongside Gropius's Bauhaus in Dessau and Le Corbusier's "League of Nations" project. Like his German colleagues, he was not *just* an architect; he always followed the idea of the complete work of art. So, almost accidentally, a number of design objects were created that today count as classics.

The focus of all of his designs was always functionality, albeit a functionality that nevertheless radiated comfort. So, quite in contrast to his design colleagues from Germany and Italy, he used natural materials instead of glass and steel. The typically soft, often irregular Aalto shapes, such as waves and folds, also became symbols for the move toward a more human functionalism.

Inspired by Breuer's cantilever chair, the Thonet chairs, and a company in Estonia that manufactured tram seats from plywood, he devoted himself to bending wood. The chair *No. 41* and the first wooden cantilever chair, *No. 31*, which would subsequently become the symbol for Scandinavia's move into a new design era, were created in his plywood workshops with the furniture manufacturer Otto Korhonen. Thanks to further innovations in the field of bentwood, which he lovingly called the "little sister of the architectonic column," over the years, further furniture ranges were developed: with L-legs (1932–33), Y-legs (1946–47), and folding legs (1954). The success of this furniture and the resulting trend toward natural materials and soft shapes enabled him to set up the ARTEK furniture company with his wife in 1935 and to submit a patent for the wooden cantilever chair.

In accordance with the principle of the complete work of art, in addition to his work as an architect and furniture designer for the houses Iittala and Riihimäki, Aalto was also a freelance designer. His most famous design also comes from this period, the *Savoy* vase from 1937, which he had designed for the Savoy Restaurant in Helsinki. The wavelike shape of this vase, which was originally called "Eskimoerindensskinnbuxa" (leather trousers worn by Eskimo women) and which is today known under the name *Aalto* vase, is based on a lakefront. The crucial aspect of the shape of the vase, which can also be considered symbolic for Aalto's other designs, is that it is both organic and abstract.

His design philosophy, which rejects both formal rationality and artificially manufactured materials, is today considered to be the basis for Scandinavian design. With his great success in the US and Great Britain, he influenced the designers there with this ideals, including the married design team Charles and Ray Eames. *nk*

1898 Born on February 3 in Kuortane, Finland
1903 Moves with his family to Jyväskylä
1916–21 Studies architecture at the Helsinki University of Technology
1923 Opens the Alvar Aalto Office for Architecture and Monumental Art
1924 Marries the architect Aino Marsio
1928 Member of the Congrès Internationaux d'Architecture Moderne (CIAM)
1933 Moves to Helsinki and sets up the furniture company ARTEK
1937 Finnish pavilion for the World's Fair in Paris; *Savoy* vase (*Aalto* vase)
1939 Finnish pavilion for the World's Fair in New York, Aalto exhibition in the MoMa (Museum of Modern Art), New York
1940–48 Professor of architecture at MIT (Massachusetts Institute of Technology) in Cambridge
1949 Death of his wife, Aino
1952 Marries the architect Elissa Mäkiniemi
1962–71 Finlandia Helsinki (Congress and Concert Center)
1976 Dies on May 11 in Helsinki

Portrait of Alvar Aalto, 1970

1902 Alfred Stieglitz founds the
Photo-Secession in New York

1929 Stock market
crash heralds
global economic
crisis

1894 Tower Bridge in London
opened for traffic

1914 Marcel Duchamp's first
readymade, *Bottle Rack*

1850   1855   1860   1865   1870   1875   1880   1885   1890   1895   1900   1905   1910   1915   1920   1925   1930   1935

1948/49 Berlin Airlift

1982 Michael Jackson, *Thriller*

1939 Germany invades Poland;
World War II commences

1992 Founding of the European Union

1973 Chilean coup d'état; elected president
Salvador Allende dies

| 1940 | 1945 | 1950 | 1955 | 1960 | 1965 | 1970 | 1975 | 1980 | 1985 | 1990 | 1995 | 2000 | 2005 | 2010 | 2015 | 2020 | 2025 |

WILHELM WAGENFELD

With the MT 8 table lamp, Wilhelm Wagenfeld successfully developed a new design form that embodied modernity during his time as a student at the Bauhaus. Wagenfeld, who was born in Bremen, is today considered a pioneer of industrial design.

Instead of "arts and crafts," the new orientation of the Bauhaus in 1922 was to create a symbiosis of "art and technology." With the Hungarian artist László Moholy-Nagy, who was director of the metal workshop from the spring of 1923, this new orientation began to take shape with a vengeance. He demanded and encouraged the development of a new language of forms, in particular through the use and unusual combination of inexpensive materials. At his suggestion, the metal workshop designed light fittings for the planned model house, the Haus am Horn. For this house, the Swiss silversmith Carl Jacob Jucker developed various lamps with glass feet and shafts, to which, in a formally not very convincing manner, he added mirrored bulbs or semicircular reflectors. Jucker's creative achievement consisted in the use of a glass shaft and the disclosure of function through the visibility of the inner wiring. Another Bauhaus student, Gyula Pap, later claimed that at that time he had placed a glass tube on Jucker's table for the building of a lamp. But the documentation shows that at that point in time Jucker had already finished designing his lamps.

In April 1924, Wilhelm Wagenfeld took his journeyman's examination as a silversmith. Again it was Moholy-Nagy who gave the stimulus for the design of lamps. Wagenfeld, who knew Jucker's experiment, which was not suitable for industrial use, created with his well-balanced concept an immediately convincing solution. He solved the problem of the reflector with a frosted glass dome, which rests on soldered metal rods that support a surrounding metal band. This design by Wagenfeld succeeded in meeting the aesthetic criteria of the Bauhaus. Foot, shaft, and dome now formed a unity, with harmonious proportions and a pleasant light effect. The lamp is not too dazzling, as the shade itself emits some light. But this was not enough. Moholy-Nagy's next step was to ensure that Wagenfeld produced his lamp in a variant material with the glass parts, also used by Carl Jucker, for the foot and shaft. Wagenfeld also moved the cable, visible in Jucker's design, enclosing it in a metal tube (MT 9 and ME1).

From 1928, the Berlin company Schwintzer & Gräff manufactured the lamp in two different sizes. In 1930, Wagenfeld himself created a variation on both lamps. The version reworked since 1980 by the Bremen firm of Tecnolumen together with Wagenfeld corresponds, apart from minimal alterations such as the diameter of the base, to the original version. It was precisely through the design boom of the 1980s that the Bauhaus lamps are now modernist classics, and remain paradigmatic for the entire Bauhaus aesthetic. *js*

1900 Born on April 15
1914–18 Apprenticeship as industrial designer at the silverware company Koch & Bergfeld in Bremen
1916–19 Kunstgewerbeschule Bremen
1919–22 Trains at the Zeichenakademie Hanau
1923–25 Works at the metal workshop of the Bauhaus Weimar under László Moholy-Nagy
1924 Final examination as silversmith
1926–30 Assistant, from 1928 head of the metal workshop of the Bauhochschule Weimar
1930–35 Freelancer, main client Glaswerk Schott & Gen in Jena
1931–35 Professor at the Staatlichen Kunsthochschule Grunewaldstraße Berlin
FROM 1935 Artistic director at Vereinigten Lausitzer Glaswerke in Weißwasser, Oberlausitz
1947–49 Professor of industrial design at the Hochschule für Bildende Kunst Berlin
1954–78 "Werkstatt Wagenfeld" in Stuttgart
1990 Dies in Stuttgart

left page
Wilhelm Wagenfeld, Bauhaus lamp, metal version, Bauhaus Weimar, 1924

above
Portrait of Wilhelm Wagenfeld, 1920s

1901 André Malraux, French Minister
of Culture, is born

1870/71 Franco-Prussian War

1889 Vincent van Gogh, *Starry Night*

1916–1922 Dadaist
movement

| 1850 | 1855 | 1860 | 1865 | 1870 | 1875 | 1880 | 1885 | 1890 | 1895 | 1900 | 1905 | 1910 | 1915 | 1920 | 1925 | 1930 | 1935 |

Jean Prouvé, Wall lamp Potence, 1950,
re-edition by Vitra

1940   1945   1950   1955   1960   1965   1970   1975   1980   1985   1990   1995   2000   2005   2010   2015   2020   2025

JEAN PROUVÉ

Jean Prouvé, wrought-iron craftsman, designer, product developer, and architect, is one of the central figures of 20th-century design. His background as a metalsmith enabled him to create innovative furniture designs.

"Prouvé was indissolubly an architect and an engineer, or even better, an architect and a master builder, since everything he touches and designs immediately takes on an elegant, beautiful form while he finds brilliant solutions to resistance and manufacturing."

This was how Le Corbusier evaluated the work of the great designer and engineer. However, in spite of his countless construction projects, Prouvé could never call himself an architect because of his lack of formal training. As a design engineer, he created prototypes of industrial designs, from facades to roof constructions to different house types. His most significant construction is the *Maison du peuple* in Clichy (1935–39) with its modern curtain wall. As a furniture designer, we still have Prouvé to thank for style icons such as the *Cité* chair, which he created in 1930 for a competition to furnish a student apartment in the Cité Universitaire in Nancy.

The trademarks for Jean Prouvé are his simple but efficient designs. As a trained metal artisan, he treasured the clarity of technical objects and recognized the aesthetic possibilities in the different materials he used in his designs. Even the first furniture designs are thought out in detail and manufactured so that the construction itself becomes a specific design element: screws and joints remain just as visible as the traces of the manufacturing process that he deliberately leaves. From 1923 on, in his own workshop in Nancy, Prouvé created not just the first furniture designs but also rails, metal separating walls and doors, glazing, balustrades, lighting fixtures, sliding windows, and elevator cars made of sheet steel – engineering systems and construction parts, many of which received their own patents. The cool and functional aesthetics of the sheet-steel furniture, which Prouvé exhibited for the first time in 1925 at the *Exposition Internationale des Arts Décoratifs et Industriels Modernes* in Paris, drew the attention of the architects Le Corbusier, Pierre Jeanneret, and Robert

Mallet-Steven, for whom he developed constructive solutions to their construction requirements.

After Prouvé received his first significant order – the design of the entrance gate of the Villa Reifenberg for Robert Stevens-Mallet – the commissions for his engineering design ideas did not stop. From 1931 to 1939, Prouvé worked with the architects Tony Garnier, Eugène Beaudouin, and Marcel Gabriel Lods, with whom he constructed the aviation club Roland Garros in Buc and also the prototype of a weekend house. His invention of the school desk and chair combination caused a sensation. In the 1950s, in collaboration with Charlotte Perriand, he created bookshelves made of wood and sheet metal with irregularly arranged compartments into which brightly painted back walls and sheet metal doors were inserted. Furniture production came to an abrupt halt in 1953, when Prouvé was forced out of the Ateliers Jean Prouvé factory, which he had founded, by the majority owner Aluminium Français.

However, with his own engineering design company Les Constructions Jean Prouvé, established in Paris with Michel Bataille, he continued to create self-contained architectural works: in 1955, the house for himself and his family in Nancy constructed from remnants of his former factory; that same year, a giant pavilion on the bank of the River Seine in Paris for the 100th anniversary of the invention of aluminum; in 1956, the prototype of a prefabricated house for the homeless program run by the "Emmaus" founder, Abbé Pierre; and in 1957, the Evian pump room on Lake Geneva.

In addition to furniture, buildings and numerous patents, Prouvé's complete works also include his legendary teaching activity at the renowned Conservatoire National des Arts et Métiers (CNAM) in Paris from 1958 to 1971.

In 1971, as one of the judges for the construction competition for the Centre Pompidou, Prouvé was able to push through the bold design by the young architects Renzo Piano and Richard Rogers. *hd*

1901 Born on April 8 in Paris
1916–21 Trains as a wrought-iron craftsman
1924 Opens his own workshop
1925 First sheet-steel furniture
1930 Founding member of the Union des Artists Modernes (UAM) group of artists
1931 Establishes the design engineering company Les Ateliers de Jean Prouvé
1947 Constructs the Maxéville factory (200 employees)
1953 Leaves company after rows with the majority shareholder
1954 Design and construction of own house in Nancy
1956 Establishes design engineering office Les Constructions Jean Prouvé (together with Michel Bataille) in Paris
1968–84 Office in Paris as a freelance architect
1984 Dies on March 23 in Nancy

Portrait of Jean Prouvé

1919 Bauhaus founded by
Walter Gropius in Weimar

1895 First Venice Biennale

1911 Wassily Kandinsky,
Impression III

1929 Stock market
crash heralds
global economic
crisis

1850   1855   1860   1865   1870   1875   1880   1885   1890   1895   1900   1905   1910   1915   1920   1925   1930   1935

1950–1953 Korean War

1970 Robert Smithson, *Spiral Jetty*

1988 *Freeze*, exhibition of the Young British Artists group in London

1940–1944 Vichy regime in France

1961 John F. Kennedy sworn in as president of the US

1993–1997 Frank O. Gehry, Guggenheim Museum, Bilbao

1940 1945 1950 1955 1960 1965 1970 1975 1980 1985 1990 1995 2000 2005 2010 2015 2020 2025

MARCEL BREUER

According to legend, the handlebars of his bicycle were the inspiration for his most famous design, the cantilever chairs. Breuer became the master of tubular steel frame chairs.

Walter Gropius considered Marcel Breuer to be his most talented student. Many of his furniture designs came from the period at the Bauhaus school and they display the detached elegance and practicality for which the German designer became famous. His *Wassily Chair* is one of the best-known chairs of modern times and is also one of the most copied designs.

In 1920, Marcel Breuer arrived at the Bauhaus school in Weimar and became director of the furniture workshop when he was still a junior master. He designed furniture based on a rational simplification in the style of his teacher, Gropius. He created classic pieces of furniture for modern times. They were distinctive with their lightness and geometric forms and corresponded with functional principles. First it was wooden furniture that was designed with simple, geometric shapes in the style of the Bauhaus. Then, when Breuer discovered the design opportunities of Mannesmann tubular steel, he brought the light, metallic, gleaming look to modern design. Breuer designed the *Wassily Chair* (also known as B2) for Kandinsky's home in Dessau, and in doing this he used the new materials for the first time. With the curves, the angled planes, and the materials used, the construction is modern as well as inviting and comfortable. The subsequent experiments and research into tubular steel furniture led in 1928 to the first cantilever chair, a chair without rear legs. In time, a whole series of tubular steel furniture was created, including tables, stools, and cupboards, which all utilized the benefits of tubular steel: low costs, hygiene, durability, and comfort.

Breuer designed the interior decoration and furnishings for the new Bauhaus school in Dessau, where he taught until 1928. He then managed his own architecture company in Berlin and continued to design furniture and interior decoration there while his architectural designs mainly remained on the shelf. In 1935, like many of his Bauhaus colleagues, he emigrated. His first stop was London,

where he worked with the architect FRS Yorke and became director of the design department at Isokon. Inspired by Aalto's laminate wood designs, which were exhibited in London from 1933 on, Breuer began to transfer his tubular steel constructions to laminate wood for the first time.

In 1937, Marcel Breuer then followed the call of Walter Gropius to Harvard. His professorship for architecture also symbolized the change in his career, as from now on he concentrated mainly on building designs. He also founded an architecture agency with Gropius and together they established the Bauhaus style in America. The Alan I. W. Frank house in Pittsburgh, which was designed as a complete work of art, including interior design and furniture, is an impressive relic from this period.

Their collaborative work ended in 1941. Breuer set up his own architecture agency, Marcel Breuer & Associates, which he relocated to New York in 1947. In the 1950s, like Le Corbusier, he worked mainly with concrete, and with his later giant buildings, such as the Whitney Museum of Modern Art and the UNESCO headquarters in Paris, he became a forerunner of Brutalism. *nk*

1902 Born on May 21 in Pécs, Hungary
UNTIL 1920 Studies at the Akademie der Bildenden Künste in Vienna
1920–23 Studies at the Bauhaus Weimar, master carpenter
1925–28 Manages the furniture workshop at the Bauhaus in Dessau
1928 Sets up an architecture agency in Berlin
1935 Emigrates to England; collaborates with the architect FRS Yorke, designs for Isokon
1937 Emigrates to the US, architecture agency with Walter Gropius in Cambridge, professorship at the Harvard School of Architecture
1956 Architecture agency Marcel Breuer & Associates in New York
1981 Dies in New York

left page
Marcel Breuer, D4 armchair, Bauhaus Dessau, 1927, re-edition by TECTA, Lauenförde

above
Portrait of Marcel Breuer

left
Bauhaus display cases, 1925,
re-edition by TECTA, Lauenförde

right page
Container S41, S43, 1924/27,
re-edition by TECTA, Lauenförde

1901 Queen Victoria dies **1913** Armory Show in New York shows
the European avant-garde

1891 Construction of Trans-Siberian
Railway begins

1928 Alexander Fleming
discovers penicillin

1906 San Francisco earthquake

1850 1855 1860 1865 1870 1875 1880 1885 1890 1895 1900 1905 1910 1915 1920 1925 1930 1935

left
Arne Jacobsen, Ant chair, models 3101, 1952,
re-edition by Fritz Hansen, Allerød

next double page
Egg visitor chair, model 3316, 1958

1939–1945 World War II

1959 Completion of the Solomon
R. Guggenheim Museum in
New York

1965 First Op Art exhibition,
The Responsive Eye in New York

1976 Apple Computers founded

1992 Maastricht Treaty establishes
the EU

1999 First e-book reader

| 1940 | 1945 | 1950 | 1955 | 1960 | 1965 | 1970 | 1975 | 1980 | 1985 | 1990 | 1995 | 2000 | 2005 | 2010 | 2015 | 2020 | 2025 |

ARNE JACOBSEN

His understanding of how to harmonize geometric forms and organically flowing lines, classical proportions, and modern visions is unrivaled. With his seating furniture, which had naturalistic names such as Ant, Egg, *and* Swan, *he created the design icons of the 20th century.*

Yet Arne Jacobsen himself, one of the most influential Scandinavian designers of the 20th century, resisted the term "designer." Although he created timeless modern seating furniture such as the *Egg* and the *Seven*, he always saw himself as an architect. In fact, outside of Denmark, his architectural work, which includes private residences and settlements as well as public buildings, has rather unjustly taken a backseat. His constructions were part of the pioneering achievements of Scandinavian modern art before World War II. His visionary designs for the circular *House of the Future* (1929), a flat-roofed building constructed of glass and concrete with a heliport, and the *Bellavista* settlement (1931–34) in particular made Jacobsen a forerunner of the International Style.

In the 1950s and 1960s, Arne Jacobsen consistently implemented the idea of "architecture as a complete work of art." His integrated approach meant that he devoted meticulous attention to even the smallest details of interior decoration as well as to furniture, lamps, and textiles. His masterpiece was the SAS Royal Hotel in Copenhagen. Everything here bears the mark of Jacobsen, from the architecture of the skyscraper, which is almost 70 meters tall (at that time the tallest building in the country), to the door handles, ashtrays, candlesticks, and the *AJ* stainless-steel cutlery in the restaurant. Until then, an abundance of gold, marble, and red velvet had been synonymous with luxury hotels; Jacobsen, however, set completely new standards.

Even the architecture – a 20-story building with a curtain wall made of glass and steel – illustrated that fact that Arne Jacobsen was striving for a radical modern concept. The building, the interior, and the furnishings were intended to form a consistent whole, and so for the lobby and reception areas, Jacobsen designed the *Egg* and *Swan* seats, created as modern plastic shells with cold foam upholstery and an aluminum stand. Both chairs were created without straight lines, and with their organic, flowing shapes they form a fascinating contrast to the otherwise strictly geometric lines of the hotel. With its high back and the protruding sides, the *Egg* is a new interpretation of the wing chair and offers a private space in the public room of the reception area. Like the other seating furniture by Jacobsen, the chairs are still produced by the Danish furniture company Fritz Hansen.

Arne Jacobsen had already won a silver medal at the *Exposition Internationale des Arts Décoratifs* in Paris in 1925 with the design for a chair. His most famous chair, however, is probably the *Ant*, which he designed for Fritz Hansen in 1952. The laminated wooden chair takes its name from the strongly tapered backrest and the three or four thin, steel-tube legs. Three years later, he developed *Chair 3107 – Series 7*, which had a simplified backrest. Compact, light, and stackable and available with or without armrests and in a variety of colors, the *Seven* was perfect for modern living and became a huge success. To date, more than five million units have been sold. It is one of the most copied chairs in the world. *ch*

1902 Born in Copenhagen
AROUND 1922–24 Apprenticeship as
a stonemason
1924–27 Studies architecture at the
Royal Danish Academy of Fine
Arts in Copenhagen
1925 Works on the Danish pavilion
for the Paris World Exhibition;
silver medal for chair design
1927–29 Works at the planning
office for the Copenhagen local
authority
1929 Own architecture office in
Hellerup; designs the *House of
the Future* for a competition
(together with Flemming Lassen)
1931 Rothenborg House, Klampenborg
1931–34 Bellavista settlement in
Copenhagen
1943–45 Flees to Sweden before
Denmark is occupied by the
Nazi Germany
1952 *Ant* chair
1956–61 SAS Royal Hotel with the
Egg and *Swan* chairs
1956–65 Professor of architecture
at the Academy of Fine Arts in
Copenhagen
1969–63 St. Catherine's College,
Oxford
1971 Dies in Copenhagen

left
Swan chair in Fritz Hansen's headquarters in Allerød, models 3320, 1958,
re-edition by Fritz Hansen, Allerød

above
Portrait of Arne Jacobsen

1904 "Entente cordiale" between the
United Kingdom and France

1925 Francis Scott Fitzgerald,
The Great Gatsby

1912 Jackson Pollock
is born

| 1850 | 1855 | 1860 | 1865 | 1870 | 1875 | 1880 | 1885 | 1890 | 1895 | 1900 | 1905 | 1910 | 1915 | 1920 | 1925 | 1930 | 1935 |

1937–1945 Second Sino-Japanese War

1957 Soviet Union launches the first *Sputnik*

1972 US uses napalm as a tool of war in Vietnam

1993 Nelson Mandela and F. W. de Klerk awarded Nobel Peace Prize

1945 Beginning of Cold War

1968 Assassination of Martin Luther King

1983 Discovery of the AIDS virus, HIV

2003 Human genome project completed

| 1940 | 1945 | 1950 | 1955 | 1960 | 1965 | 1970 | 1975 | 1980 | 1985 | 1990 | 1995 | 2000 | 2005 | 2010 | 2015 | 2020 | 2025 |

ISAMU NOGUCHI

Isamu Noguchi, sculptor, product designer, set designer, landscape architect, and designer, ranks among the most influential artistic personalities of the 20th century.

Isamu Noguchi is one of the most interesting figures at the interface of 20th-century art and design. Stimulated by very diverse areas and genres, he created far-reaching works that comprised not only sculptural work in the minimalist tradition but also the design of lights, furniture, stage sets, and public areas. He thus managed to build a bridge between visual and applied art, between East and West, between artistic vision and practical function.

Born the son of the American author Léonie Gilmour and the Japanese poet Yonejiro (Yone) Noguchi in 1904, Isamu experienced the tension of two cultures that could not be more different. He grew up in Japan from 1906 to 1918 and then attended school in the US. In 1922, he began a medical degree but very soon abandoned it in order to study sculpture.

A Guggenheim scholarship enabled him to travel to Paris in 1927, where he worked under Constantin Brâncuşi. In 1928, he returned to New York and set up a studio there. Further trips to Europe and Asia brought him into contact with Japanese calligraphy and pottery, among other things. In New York, this commuter between East and West got to know the choreographer Martha Graham and a productive cooperation developed between the two. Until the mid-1960s, Noguchi was to design 21 stage sets for Graham, the outstanding representative of modern dance theater – including such productions as *Herodiade* (1944) and *Judith* (1950). In the 1940s, Noguchi designed a series of light sculptures made of paper (*Lunar*). From 1951 on, he created the famous *Akari* paper lanterns for which Noguchi revived the ancient Japanese art of making paper from the bark of the mulberry tree. *Akari* is the Japanese term for lightness and light: "The light of Akari is like the light of the sun filtered through the paper of *shoji*. The hardness of electricity is thus transformed through the magic of paper back to the light of our origin – the sun – so that its warmth may continue to fill our rooms at night." (Isamu Noguchi)

In the 1940s and 1950s, Noguchi designed his most famous pieces of furniture: the *Coffee Table*, whose heavy glass plate rests on an organic, curved, sculptural foot, the ingenious *Chess Table*, and the filigree *Rocking Stool* (1954).

Noguchi's sculptures also serve a purpose: the *Garden Seat* (1963), for example, made of basalt or granite, and the *Water Table* (1968) have recesses to collect rainwater so that birds can drink from them.

For his art projects in the public arena, Noguchi frequently worked with architects, such as the railing for two bridges (1951) for the Hiroshima Peace Park and *Sunken Garden* for the library of Yale University (1960–64).

In the 1970s and 1980s, he added further large-scale garden projects: UNESCO Paris, 1956–58; Billy Rose Sculpture Garden, Israel Museum, Jerusalem, 1960–65; Bayfront Park, Miami, Florida, 1978; California Scenario, Costa Mesa, California; Domon Ken Museum Garden, Skata, Japan, 1984, and the Moere-Ken Park Sapporo, Japan, 1988.

In the years from 1981 to 1985, Noguchi constructed his own museum, the Isamu Noguchi Garden Museum in Long Island City, New York. In all genres, the works of Noguchi are impressive with their timeless, Asian-influenced aesthetics, which are often close to biomorphic abstraction or minimal art but which also embody the Japanese tradition. hd

1904 Born on November 17 in Los Angeles
1906 Grows up in Japan until 1918 and then returns to the USA
1922 Starts a medical degree, but soon devotes himself exclusively to sculpture
1927 Guggenheim scholarship, assistant to Constantin Brâncuşi in Paris
1929 Start of cooperation with Martha Graham in New York
1937 Initial industrial design: *Zenith Radio Nurse*
1950 Designs the Hiroshima Memorial Park
1951 Starts work on the *Akari* paper lanterns
1956 Works on the garden for UNESCO in Paris
1960 Designs the gardens for Yale University and for the Israel Museum in Jerusalem
1968 Retrospective at the Whitney Museum, New York; autobiography *A Sculptor's World*
1985 Opening of the Isamu Noguchi Garden Museum, Long Island City, New York
1988 Dies in New York

left page
Isamu Noguchi, coffee table, 1944, re-edition by Vitra

above
Portrait of Isamu Noguchi

1919 Treaty of Versailles officially
ends World War I

1909 Opening of Queensboro
Bridge in New York

1930 Grant Wood,
American Gothi

1850	1855	1860	1865	1870	1875	1880	1885	1890	1895	1900	1905	1910	1915	1920	1925	1930	1935

Charles and Ray Eames, La Chaise, 1948,
re-edition by Vitra

1944 Normandy landings

1956 Elvis Presley has his first major hit, *Heartbreak Hotel*

1969 Stonewall riots on Christopher Street in New York

1990 End of Cold War

1981 Ronald Reagan sworn in as 40th president of the US

2003 US invasion of Iraq

1949 The Soviet Union commences its first atomic test

1962 Andy Warhol, *Campbell's Soup Cans*

1973 First commercial personal computer

1940 1945 1950 1955 1960 1965 1970 1975 1980 1985 1990 1995 2000 2005 2010 2015 2020 2025

CHARLES & RAY EAMES

The spirit of optimism in America after World War II made modern design accessible to a wider audience. Ray and Charles Eames did not just experiment with new technologies and materials in furniture design – laminated wood, plastic, steel wire, and aluminum – they also displayed their versatility with innovative architecture and film projects.

They were not the first to experiment with molded plywood, however Charles Eames and his congenial partner and wife, Ray, were able to literally bend the wood into new shapes and change furniture design of the 20th century forever with their designs. In 1941, in their apartment in Los Angeles, the newly married couple set up a workshop with their home-made plywood press – the *Kazam!* Machine – named for the magic spell "Ala Kazam!" (hocus pocus). Of course it was not magic; it was heat, pressure, and glue that bent the thin veneer plywood into sweeping complex curves in the press.

Charles Eames had already had his first experience of bending laminated wood at the Cranbrook Academy of Art. In 1940, together with his friend Eero Saarinen, he won first prize in the competition "Organic Design in Home Furnishings," which was awarded by the MoMA in New York. However, due to the shortage of materials in the war years, the designs could not be realized. The *Kazam!* Machine was initially also used for an order placed by the US Navy, who commissioned the Eames couple to design arm and leg splints as well as stretchers made of shaped plywood.

In the following years, their spectacular *Plywood* furniture collection for the company Herman Miller included the *Lounge Chair Wood* (*LCW*, 1945), which was constructed of several shaped pieces of plywood. By combining a seat with different frames and covers, Charles and Ray Eames created a number of variants – ideal for mass production. A further development of the *LCW* is the famous *Lounge Chair No. 670* (1956), which they designed as a contemporary version of the English club chair with dark palisander veneer, black leather upholstery, and black painted aluminum.

In addition to shaped plywood, the Eames duo also discovered fiberglass as a design material in the 1950s. Back in 1948, they designed the elegant, expansive chair sculpture *La Chaise*, which was inspired by a sculpture by the sculptor Gaston Lachaise and whose sweeping fiberglass shell rested on a chrome frame and an oak cruciform base.

Their principle, "Create the best for the most for the least," was also applied to their *Plastic Armchairs* and the *Plastic Side Chairs* (1950), which combined an organically shaped seat made of colored plastic with a variety of frames. Plastic was followed by aluminum with the elegant office chairs of the *Aluminum Group* (1958).

The Eames duo was also known for its architectural projects, in particular the *Case Study Houses No. 8 and 9* (1949). The two Eames houses, which had steel frames, were unique in their very light construction and assembly method. For the most part they were constructed out of prefabricated elements from industrial construction. "Design is the appropriate combination of materials in order to solve a problem," said Charles Eames. ch

1907 Charles Eames is born in St. Louis, Missouri
1912 Bernice Alexandra "Ray" Kaiser is born in Sacramento, California
1925 Charles receives an architecture scholarship for Washington University, St. Louis
1930 Charles opens an architecture agency in St. Louis
1933 Ray studies painting under Hans Hofmann in New York
1940 Ray starts a course at the Cranbrook Academy of Art in Michigan
1941 Charles and Ray marry and move to Los Angeles
1942 They open a design studio
1946 *Plywood Group* goes into production
1948 Charles Eames and Eero Saarinen win the MoMA "Low-Cost Furniture Competition"
1949 Construction of two of the *Case Study Houses* designed by the Eames duo in Pacific Palisades
1956 *Lounge Chair No. 670*
1958 *Aluminum Group* furniture range
1978 Charles Eames dies in Los Angeles
1988 Ray Eames dies exactly ten years to the day after the death of Charles

Portrait of Charles and Ray Eames

1917 October Revolution
in Russia

1933 Franklin
D. Roosevelt
sworn in as
president of
the US

1893 Edvard Munch, *The Scream*

1909 Publication of the
Futurist Manifesto

1850 1855 1860 1865 1870 1875 1880 1885 1890 1895 1900 1905 1910 1915 1920 1925 1930 1935

Max Bill, Ulm stool, 1955,
re-edition Manufactum

1949 Founding of the
North Atlantic
Treaty Organization

1961 Yuri Gagarin is the first
man in space

1976 First G7 summit

1996 First cloned mammal
(Dolly the sheep)

2001 Terrorist attacks on World Trade Center (9/11)

1954 Premiere of Hitchcock's film
Rear Window

1987 Black Monday (October 19) sees
stock market crash worldwide

2007 iPhone launched

1940   1945   1950   1955   1960   1965   1970   1975   1980   1985   1990   1995   2000   2005   2010   2015   2020   2025

MAX BILL

Max Bill is a "universal man" whose name is closely linked to architecture, fine art, product design, typography, journalism, research, teaching, and, with his elective office in the Swiss National Council, with politics, too.

The Swiss painter, architect, furniture designer, and art theorist was an important exponent of "concrete art," in which materials and regularity are exclusively used without any alignment to nature. For example, between 1935 and 1938, *Fifteen Variations on a Single Theme* were created, whereby a composition of primary and secondary colors was created in different arrangements. In his numerous sculptures, which were based on mathematical rules, the artist also created variations on a single theme (*Continuity*, 1983–86). From 1945 on, Bill also designed utility objects. For the company Junghans, he designed a range of clocks that have become legendary for their constructive clarity and precise proportions, and with the *Ulm Stool*, he also became known as a furniture designer.

After he abandoned a silversmithing course at the Zurich Kunstgewerbeschule, Max Bill studied architecture at the Bauhaus school in Dessau from 1927 to 1929. His teachers there included Wassily Kandinsky, Paul Klee, Oskar Schlemmer, and László Moholy-Nagy. The Bauhaus teaching gave him the idea of unifying all arts and of an art form in which the material would suit the function. However, the Dutch painter and founder of Neoplasticism, Piet Mondrian (De Stijl), whom Bill met after returning to Zurich in 1932, probably had an even greater influence on him. With Mondrian, an artist of the De Stijl movement, Bill was encouraged to accept the mathematically constructed, concrete art that used only its own resources without any reference to nature. The second important stop on the road to Dessau for Bill was Ulm, where he became one of the founders of the Ulm School of Design in 1951. He designed the buildings for the school and was its first principal from 1953 to 1956. In addition to the basic teachings, which were strongly based on the Bauhaus introductory course, there was particular focus on the development and design of industrially manufactured mass products. Some graduates of the school were subsequently employed as designers in large companies and had a significant influence on German product design, for example Dieter Rams for the company Braun. The development of the school, which was promising at first, was soon restricted by conservative powers and steered along different tracks. In 1969, it was closed for political reasons. Bill had already left the school back in 1957 to begin working as a freelance architect and artist.

In addition to his artistic activities, Bill published numerous principles on concrete art (*The Mathematical Way of Thinking in the Visual Art of Our Time*, 1949). From 1940 to 1960, Bill was concerned mainly with the design of objects with "product forms," which for him were just as important as the works of art. As an industrial product designer, Bill designed such diverse objects as typewriters, pendant lamps, sunlamps, and hairbrushes. His most famous design work is certainly the *Ulm Stool* (1954), which combines various functions: it is a stool, side table, stepladder, and transport container. In addition to his numerous artistic works – paintings, sculptures, as well as graphics – Max Bill also designed metal lights, chair and table models (*Cross-Frame Chair*, 1951), and sculptural arrangements for public areas such as *Statues – Group of Three* from 1989 in front of the Mercedes-Benz Center in Stuttgart.

From 1967 to 1974, Bill was professor of environmental design at the Hochschule für Bildende Künste in Hamburg. In 1987, a large exhibition at the Schirn-Kunsthalle in Frankfurt am Main followed and in 1990/91, the Wilhelm-Hack-Museum held a retrospective of the artist. *hd*

1908 Born on December 22 in
Moosseedorf, near Bern
1924–27 Studies at the Kunstgewerbeschule in Zurich
1927–29 Studies at the Bauhaus
Dessau
1929 Moves to Zurich; works as
architect, painter, sculptor,
graphic designer, and journalist
1926–32 Member of the Parisian artist
group "abstraction-création"
FROM 1938 Member of the CIAM
1951–53 Establishes and designs the
buildings for the Hochschule für
Gestaltung in Ulm
1953–56 First principal of the Ulm
School of Design
1967–74 Professor of environmental
design at the Hochschule für
Bildende Künste in Hamburg
1994 Dies on December 9 in Berlin

Portrait of Max Bill, 1969

1922 First British Mount
Everest Expedition

1911 Marie Curie awarded the
Nobel Prize for Chemistry

| 1850 | 1855 | 1860 | 1865 | 1870 | 1875 | 1880 | 1885 | 1890 | 1895 | 1900 | 1905 | 1910 | 1915 | 1920 | 1925 | 1930 | 1935 |

Eero Saarinen, Tulip chair, 1956

1940 Charlie Chaplin,
      The Great Dictator

1952 Elvis Presley becomes famous

1963 Martin Luther King's
     "I have a dream" speech

1978 The Galápagos Islands are
     the first item on the UNESCO
     World Heritage list

1986 First modular space station *Mir*;
     Challenger space shuttle disaster

1995 Japanese electronic pet
     Tamagotchi launched

2000 Dot-com bubble bursts

2004 Facebook set up

2010 Earthquake in Haiti
     kills 220,000

1940   1945   1950   1955   1960   1965   1970   1975   1980   1985   1990   1995   2000   2005   2010   2015   2020   2025

EERO SAARINEN

As the son of the famous Finnish architect Eliel Saarinen, his talent was predestined. Just as significant as his architectural works, however, are his organic furniture designs for Knoll International, in particular the one-legged Tulip Chair, which won numerous awards.

Eero Saarinen's architectural masterpiece is the TWA Terminal at New York's JFK airport; his greatest triumph in the field of design is the *Tulip Chair*. If one considers the flowing, curved lines of the departure hall and the sculpturally shaped seat of the *Tulip Chair*, one is struck by their expressive, organic design, which was futuristic-looking in those days. It was thus with good reason that a slightly modified version of the *Tulip Chair* found itself on the set of the spaceship Enterprise in the science-fiction television series *Star Trek*.

For Eero Saarinen, who was born in Finland, architecture was always his "main occupation." At the same time, however, he was also fascinated with the idea that no piece of work can be viewed in isolation and that each part of a work reflects and supplements the other parts. His credo was: "Always design a thing by considering it in its next larger context – a chair in a room, a room in a house, a house in an environment, an environment in a city plan."

The influences were already evident in his childhood. The son of the famous architect Eliel Saarinen was 13 when his family emigrated to the US. His father worked as an architect and director of the Cranbook Academy of Arts in Michigan, a type of American Bauhaus. After studying architecture, Eero Saarinen met Charles Eames in Cranbrook and the two men experimented together with new furniture shapes and materials. In 1940, they both entered several designs in the "Organic Design in Home Furnishings" competition for the Museum of Modern Art in New York. With their revolutionary seat groups made of organically shaped laminate wood, whose seats reflected the seating requirements of the human body, they moved furniture design in a new direction.

In the 1940s, Florence Knoll asked her childhood and university friend Eero Saarinen to design chairs for her husband's furniture company. In a portrait of the trendsetting furniture company Knoll Interna-

tional, *Der Spiegel* reported in 1960 that "the seat, back, and armrests were merged as if someone had sat in the snow and left an imprint of his body." Saarinen subsequently developed a range of organically shaped seating furniture such as the expansive *Womb Chair* (1946). Saarinen modeled the chair, from which the back and armrests emerge, on a foam-covered plastic shell with loose seat and back cushions.

In 1955, at the peak of his career, Saarinen designed a revolutionary collection of plastic chairs and tables with a central leg. The *Tulip Chair* consists of a white, plastic frame that rises from a column foot like the goblet of a wine glass or a tulip. Although it appears to be constructed from one piece, the base of the chair is manufactured in aluminum casting and painted. The one-legged chairs and accompanying table, which also has one leg, were Saarinen's ingenious attempt to "clear up the slum of legs in the US home," as he put it. *ch*

1910 Born in Kirkkonummi, Finland
1923 Family emigrates to the US
1929–30 Studies sculpture at the Académie de la Grande Chaumière in Paris
1930–34 Studies architecture at the Yale School of Art and Architecture
1935 Joins the architecture company of his father, Eliel Saarinen, in Cranbrook
1940 Participates (with Charles Eames) in the competition run by the Museum of Modern Art in New York. Prizes for several of their designs, including the *Organic Chair*
1946 *Womb Chair*
1949–56 General Motors Technical Center, Warren, Michigan
1950 Opens his own architecture company in Birmingham, Michigan
1952–62 TWA Terminal (TWA Flight Center) at John F. Kennedy Airport, New York
1955 *Tulip Chair*
1958–62 Dulles International Airport, Washington, D.C.
1961 Dies in Ann Arbor, Michigan

Portrait of Eero Saarinen

1922 Discovery of
Tutankhamun's
Tomb

1850   1855   1860   1865   1870   1875   1880   1885   1890   1895   1900   1905   1910   1915   1920   1925   1930   1935

Tapio Wirkkala, laminated birch
leaf dish, 1951

1938 Otto Hahn and Fritz Strassmann
discover nuclear fission

1945 End of World War II

1955 Rosa Louise Parks sparks the
Montgomery Bus Boycott

1973 Chilean coup d'état; elected
president Salvador Allende dies

1963 Assassination of John F. Kennedy

1985 Mikhail Gorbachev becomes
General Secretary of the CPSU

2004 Disastrous floods in Asia

1994 End of apartheid in South Africa

1999 Columbine High School massacre

2009 Barack Obama sworn in
as first African-American
president of the US

1940 1945 1950 1955 1960 1965 1970 1975 1980 1985 1990 1995 2000 2005 2010 2015 2020 2025

TAPIO WIRKKALA

A finely veined leaf, a drop of water, shimmering ice — throughout his life, nature was the greatest source of inspiration for Tapio Wirkkala, the father of Finnish design. Whether in his designs for glass, ceramics, metal, or wood, he managed to break down the barriers between fine arts, handicraft, and industrial production.

After studying sculpture in the mid-1930s, Tapio Wirkkala soon made his name internationally as a graphic and industrial designer. From vases and cutlery to furniture, bank notes, and stamps, his range could hardly be broader and was always accompanied by the variety of shapes in nature. The designer was particularly inspired by the raw beauty of the Finnish countryside. He spent a lot of time abroad – working from around 1955 to 1956 for the design agency of Raymond Loewy in New York – yet he often returned to Lapland. The landscape of forests and lakes, snow and ice had a lasting influence on his designs.

In 1946, Wirkkala won first prize in a design competition run by the Iittala glass company and this established his international career. It was also the start of a lifelong productive collaboration with the Finnish glassworks and he made a significant contribution to their fame. It was here between 1946 and 1960 that he produced his famous *Kantarelli* range of vases (1946). Resembling chanterelles, these handblown, cup-shaped vases open upward while fine lines run vertically through the body of the vase like the segments of a mushroom.

During his time as artistic director of the Central School of Artistic Design in Helsinki (1951–54), Wirkkala made Finnish design famous throughout the world at the Milan Trienniale exhibitions of 1951 and 1954 with his organic, natural shapes. His design of the Finnish Pavilion for 1951 was sensational. In the same year, the American magazine *House Beautiful* voted his leaf-shaped wooden bowl the "Most Beautiful Object of the Year." He created laminate wood that was then cut into a precise shape to give the object the striped effect reminiscent of the veins of a leaf.

Wirkkala was henceforth considered a "poet of wood and glass." For the carafes and glasses in the *Ultima Thule* range (1968), he was inspired by the ice melt in Lapland. Wirkkala broke new ground with his collaboration with the Venetian glass manufacturer

Venini. Many of his glass designs were typically Nordic – thick-walled and robust, as if carved out of ice – but here, the glassblowing tradition from Murano took center stage. For the two-color collection *Bolle*, he and the glassblower masters from Venini experimented with the age-old incalmo technique, whereby two glass bulbs are blown in a mold, then cut and fused together directly at the edges.

Wirkkala also very successfully designed porcelain for the Rosenthal company for many decades. His designs for the *Finlandia*, *Variation*, and *Century* ranges are still regarded as classics. In the 1960s, he also designed a range of consumer items, including plastic ketchup bottles, a glass bottle for the vodka brand Finlandia, as well as onboard cutlery and crockery for the Finnair airline.

The combination of functionality and outstanding aesthetics, of highly skilled craftsmanship and industrial production, and, not least, organic natural shapes characterize Wirkkala's designs. *ch*

1915 Born in Hanko, Finland

1933–36 Studies sculpture at the Central School for Industrial Design in Helsinki

1945 Marries the artist Rut Bryk

1946 Wins the design competition for glass art run by the company Iittala

1951 Participates in the IX Milan Trienniale

1951–54 Artistic director at the Central School for Industrial Design in Helsinki

1954 Participates in the X Milan Trienniale

1955–56 Works at Raymond Loewy's design agency in New York

1956–82 Collaborates with the Rosenthal porcelain company; collaborates with the Venetian glass company Venini

1967 *Ultima Thule* sculpture for the Montreal Expo

1971 Honorary doctorate from the Royal College of Art, London

1985 Dies in Esbo, Finland

Portrait of Tapio Wirkkala

above
Tapio glasses

right page
Kantarelli vase, 1946

1922 Joseph Stalin becomes General
Secretary of the Central
Committee of the Communist
Party of the Soviet Union

1932 Aldous Huxle
Brave New Wo

1850 1855 1860 1865 1870 1875 1880 1885 1890 1895 1900 1905 1910 1915 1920 1925 1930 1935

Lucienne Day, Calyx textile,
1951, Victoria and Albert
Museum, London

1954 First commercial nuclear
power plant in Obninsk
near Moscow

1971 Aswan Dam finished

2002 US opens detention camp
in Guantánamo

1991 Soviet coup d'etat attempt

2011 Fukushima nuclear disaster

1948 Declaration of Independence **1964** Racial segregation
of the State of Israel, May 14   abolished in the U.S.

1980–1988 First Persian Gulf War

2007–2010 Global financial crisis

1940 1945 1950 1955 1960 1965 1970 1975 1980 1985 1990 1995 2000 2005 2010 2015 2020 2025

LUCIENNE & ROBIN DAY

The furniture designer Robin Day and his wife, the textile designer Lucienne Day, caused a stir in British design of the postwar period. He created low-cost furniture, she created vivid patterns.

With their pioneering working in the field of industrial design, Lucienne and Robin Day became England's most celebrated designer couple of the postwar period. They met at the Royal College of Art and from then on they used their creative synergies both in private and for their work. They were consequently also often compared with their American contemporaries Charles and Ray Eames, although their working methods were completely different. While Charles and Ray Eames worked on their designs together, Robin and Lucienne were always lord and lady of their own areas. He designed low-cost furniture, she devoted herself to textiles, wallpaper, and carpets. The fascinating aspect of their designs is that when they are viewed together, they blend so well that they appear to have been created by the same person.

From the very start, Robin Day had the idea of creating comfortable, long-lasting yet low-cost furniture. His first success was a storage system created from plywood, for which he won first prize in the "International Competition for Low-Cost Furniture Design" in 1948 run by the Museum of Modern Art in New York. This prize led to his first commission: to design the chairs for the Royal Albert Hall.

His masterpiece, the *Polyprop* stacking chair, for which he received an OBE (Order of the British Empire) in 1983, was developed between 1962 and 1963. Inspired by the "Plastic Shell" chairs by Charles and Ray Eames, he created a chair with bent tubular steel legs and a seat shell created from a single piece of molded plastic. Robin Day was one of the first people to use polypropylene for furniture. It is extremely hard-wearing and cheap and also permits an injection-molding process in which up to 4,000 seat shells per week can be molded. It is hardly surprising that since production started in 1963, an estimated 50 million of these chairs have been sold. The success prompted Robin Day to create a complete "Polyprop family," including an

armchair (1967), the *School* chair (1971, also known as the *E-Series*), and the more extravagent *Polo* chair (1975).

Lucienne Day's abstract, colorful designs captured the spirit of the postwar years and were trendsetting in the 1950s. She was inspired both by nature as well as by the modern art of Joan Miró, Wassily Kandinsky, and Paul Klee. Her revolutionary textile design *Calyx*, which Lucienne created for the Festival of Britain, was an abstract reduction of plant motifs arranged with thin lines and irregular curved shapes.

The 1950s and 1960s in particular were very productive. During this period, she designed wallpaper, tableware, and carpets and continued to design textiles for Heals, who had produced her first design, *Calyx*. In the 1960s, her designs, which were at first rather cheerful, became simpler and more daring, for example the *Pennycress* design from 1966 and *Helix* from 1970. She wrote several books on design and received awards, including from the Council of Industrial Design and the American Institute of Decorations. Lucienne Day is thus not just one of the most important textile designers of the postwar period but also one of the few women to receive international recognition for her creative work. *nk*

1915 Robin Day is born in High Wycombe, Buckinghamshire, Great Britain

1917 Lucienne Conradi is born in Coulsdon, Surrey, Great Britain

1938 Robin graduates from the Royal College of Art, London

1940 Lucienne graduates from the Royal College of Art, London

1942 Marriage

1948 They open their design agency together; Robin: 1st prize in the "International Competition for Low-Cost Furniture Design" for the MoMa, New York

1951 Lucienne: textile design *Calyx* for the Festival of Britain

1983 Order of the British Empire (OBE) for Robin Day

2010 Lucienne dies January 30; Robin dies Novemver 9

Portrait of Robin and Lucienne Day

SORI YANAGI _____

SALVADOR DALÍ _____

ROBERT RAUSCHENBERG _____

1925 Invention of
television

1908 Child Emperor Pu Yi ascends the
Chinese throne at the age of two

1850	1855	1860	1865	1870	1875	1880	1885	1890	1895	1900	1905	1910	1915	1920	1925	1930	1935

Sori Yanagi, Butterfly stool, 1954,
re-edition by Vitra

1939–1945 World War II

1975 Pol Pot comes to power
in Cambodia

1995 *Toy Story* is first movie produced entirely
with computer animation

1966 Barnett Newman, *Who's Afraid
of Red, Yellow and Blue*

1985 Live Aid concert
for Africa

2008 Summer Olympics in
Beijing, China

2001 First same-sex "marriage" in Holland

| 1940 | 1945 | 1950 | 1955 | 1960 | 1965 | 1970 | 1975 | 1980 | 1985 | 1990 | 1995 | 2000 | 2005 | 2010 | 2015 | 2020 | 2025 |

SORI YANAGI

Sori Yanagi's design philosophy merges traditional Japanese craft with modern Western production techniques and universal humanism. In the 1950s, he was the first person to form a specific Japanese counterpoint to the famous Western designers.

Yanagi's conviction that beauty is created by simplicity and usability is proven by his career as a designer, which spans six decades. He reconciles objects and their function with the human need for harmony and balance. This connection is reflected strongly in his designs and is inferred by his biography.

Sori Yanagi was born in 1915 in Tokyo, the son of the leading philosopher of the Mingei folk art movement of the 1920s and 1930s, Muneyoshi Yanagi. His grandfather was a naval officer, land surveyor, mathematician, and member of parliament. Both strongly influenced Yanagi with their focus on traditional Japan. Yanagi himself attended the Academy of Fine Art in Tokyo from 1933 to 1940, where he also became familiar with the work of Le Corbusier. Following this, until 1942, he worked as an assistant to the designer and Le Corbusier student Charlotte Perriand, who had a consulting agency in Tokyo on behalf of the Japanese Ministry of Trade. He finally decided on a career as a designer and was soon successful. In 1947, he first taught at the Bunka Gaguin Institute and in 1951, he won the first and second prize in the Japan Industrial Design Contest.

In 1952, he founded the Yanagi Industrial Design Institute, where he created his most famous chair designs to date: the *Butterfly* stool, consisting of two curved pieces of plywood held together by a brass bracket, and the *Elephant Stool*, made of glass-fiber-reinforced polyester resin. Both seats are fundamentally different in their construction; with their simple production, however, they are both characterized by the same complete sensitivity for the harmony of form and material. The curved form of the *Butterfly*, reminiscent of a Japanese cabinet, became the basis for Yanagi's international success and for a shift in the public perception of design.

When he showed his designs at the XI Milan Trienniale in 1957, they were awarded the exhibition prize and were subsequently also exhibited at documenta III in Kassel in 1964. Both the MoMA in New York and the Paris Louvre have exhibited the *Butterfly*. Yanagi is thus attributed with opening international doors for industrial design as an art form, and designers are still benefiting from this today. Originally manufactured by the Tendo Mokko company, *Butterfly* and *Elephant Stool* are today produced by Vitra as design classics.

During his career, Yanagi designed everyday items as well as monumental bridges, subway stations, motorbikes, toys, and in 1972, the Olympic Torch for the Winter Games in Sapporo. In 1977, Yanagi became director of the Japanese Folk Art Museum in Tokyo and thus remained true to the concerns and tradition of Japanese arts and crafts. In 1982, he took part in the *Contemporary Vessels: How to Pour* exhibition organized by the Japanese National Museum for Modern Art. Sori Yanagi was active until the grand age of 96 and he created beautiful and useful items, always combining the virtues of craft and industrial production. He died in Tokyo in 2011. *jr*

1915 Sori Yanagi is born in Tokyo
1933–40 Attends the Academy of Fine Art in Tokyo
1940–42 Assistant to Charlotte Perriand
1951 First prize in the Japanese Industrial Design competition
1952 Establishes the Yanagi Industrial Design Institute
1954 Creates *Butterfly* and *Elephant Stool*
1957 The *Butterfly* wins the Trienniale prize in Milan
1964 Exhibition at documenta III in Kassel
1977 Yanagi becomes director of the Japanese Folk Art Museum
2011 Dies in Tokyo

Portrait of Sori Yanagi

1905 Greta Garbo is born

1929 Stock market crash heralds global economic crisis

1850   1855   1860   1865   1870   1875   1880   1885   1890   1895   1900   1905   1910   1915   1920   1925   1930   1935

1940 Trotsky murdered in Mexico

1964 Racial segregation abolished in the US

2001 Apple iPod launched

1931 Second Spanish Republic proclaimed in Madrid

1960 Clement Greenberg, *Modernist Painting*

1973 US Supreme Court legalizes abortion

1986 First modular space station *Mir*; *Challenger* space shuttle disaster

1993 Bombay bombings

2007 Al Gore awarded Nobel Peace Prize

2010 "Arab Spring" begins with protests in Tunisia

1940 1945 1950 1955 1960 1965 1970 1975 1980 1985 1990 1995 2000 2005 2010 2015 2020 2025

ETTORE SOTTSASS

"If anything will save us, it is beauty," said Ettore Sottsass, one of the most important designers of our time. His "Anti-Design" movement brought him international fame and success.

His *Valentine* has long been a legend: the Italian designer Ettore Sottsass designed the bright red typewriter, which became an icon of Pop Art at the end of the 1960s, for the company Olivetti 40 years ago — even today it can still be found in all major design museums, including the Museum of Modern Art in New York. Sottsass was perceived by the public mainly as an important representative of the postmodern era and as a member of the designer groups Memphis and Alchimia. Yet his complete works cannot be confined to the postmodern design of the 1980s. On the contrary: Sottsass was an incredibly creative artist who also grappled intensively with social issues and attentively followed the developments of his time.

Born in Innsbruck in 1917, Sottsass first followed in the footsteps of his father, a student of the Art Nouveau architect Otto Wagner, and completed an architecture degree. After graduating from the Politecnico di Torino in 1939, and following a short period of employment as an architect, Sottsass turned increasingly to design. In 1958, he began his long-term employment as a design consultant for the Olivetti company and in 1959, he designed the first electronic mainframe computer, *Elea 9003*. Countless designs for typewriters followed, including the design for possibly the most famous typewriter of the 20th century, the red *Valentine*, which was designed — in his words — "to keep lonely poets company on weekends in the country."

Influenced by Pop Art, Sottsass distanced himself more and more from the functionalism of his time and soon became an important leading figure of "radical design": in 1970, the first laminate *mobile grigi* appeared, bright yellow fiber-glass beds and mirrors. In 1972, he became a founding member of "Global Tools," a group of revolutionary architects and designers in Milan who rejected the strict formality of the Bauhaus school and committed themselves to searching for new avenues in design. A short time later, Sottsass joined the Milan studio

Alchimia, an experimental design formation run by Alessandro Mendini that became known for gaudily colored furniture in heterogeneous materials. In 1980 — at the age of 63 — he founded Sottsass Associati, a group of young designers and architects who looked after the complete image of a company (Esprit). One year later, the design group Memphis followed and significantly changed the world of design with bright, multifunctional designs. Irreverent and innovative, Sottsass and his colleagues mixed wood, plastic laminate, and glass, referenced historical elements, and used lavish ornaments. By 1985, however, Sottsass had already moved away from the pop culture of this bold designer group and returned with vigor to his Milan studio and architectural projects. Over the years, Sottsass Associati worked with architects to develop international architecture projects and completed industrial and graphic design orders for international customers. The list of successful constructions ranges from private houses in Colorado, Hawaii, Tuscany, Switzerland, Malaysia, the United Arab Emirates, and Belgium (*Birdhouse* in Interlaken, 1999) to a museum gallery in Ravenna, from a golf club with hotel in China to the Malpensa Airport in Milan. Sottsass was actively creative and innovative until the grand age of 90, and in addition to design and architecture, he also worked with glass, ceramics, and photography. *hd*

1917 Born on September 14 in Innsbruck

1935–39 Studies architecture in Turin

1950 Establishes his first own studio

1958 Start of collaboration with Olivetti

FROM 1960 Leading representative of the "Anti-Design" movement

1968 Famous design of the red typewriter *Valentine*

1980 Establishes his own company Sottsass Associati in Milan

1981 Establishes the Memphis design group

1994 Participates in the *Busstops* art project in Hanover; exhibition at the Centre Pompidou in Paris; at the Design Museum in London, 2007

2007 Dies in Milan on December 31

left page
Ettore Sottsass, Valentine, portable typewriter, design for Olivetti (with Perry King), 1981

above
Portrait of Ettore Sottsass

left page
Carlton, room divider, for Memphis, 1981

above
Königsworther Platz, bus stop Hanover,
1994

1892 First issue of *Vogue* in the US

1911 Roald Amundsen reaches the South Pole

1930 Luis Buñuel, *L'Age d'Or*

1850 1855 1860 1865 1870 1875 1880 1885 1890 1895 1900 1905 1910 1915 1920 1925 1930 1935

Achille Castiglioni, Sanluca, armchair, 1961

1941 Bruce Nauman is born

1955–1968 Civil rights movement in the US

1965 Beginning of Vietnam War

1983 Civil war breaks out in Sudan

1991 Conflict breaks out in the Balkans

1999 Columbine High School massacre

2005 Founding of YouTube

2010 Mass panic at the Love Parade in Duisburg, Germany

1940 1945 1950 1955 1960 1965 1970 1975 1980 1985 1990 1995 2000 2005 2010 2015 2020 2025

ACHILLE CASTIGLIONI

Achille Castiglioni is one of the most important contemporary Italian designers. His designs for lighting fixtures in particular had a profound influence on the design of lighting in the 20th century.

"So sophisticated and so simple – I like that!" This quote defines the design philosophy of Achille Castiglioni, who became world-famous first and foremost with his innovative lighting fixtures. His designs are distinguished by the playful medium of misuse and the pursuit of the reduced form. Functionality always has a higher priority than aesthetic requirement; for Castiglioni, however, a design object should always be both functional *and* well formed. His designs are highlights in the history of modern design.

At the age of 26, Achille Castiglioni, who was born in Milan, joined the architectural company run by his brothers, Livio and Pier Giacomo. Architecture, exhibition, and object designs were the focus of the family trio, which existed in this form until 1952. After Livio Castiglioni left to work alone, Achille worked with Pier Giacomo on all projects until the latter's death in 1968. The cooperation of Pier Giacomo and Achille Castiglione was highly productive over many years. With this congenial team spirit, they developed numerous innovative designs. In 1957, they first showed their design for a stool at the *Colori e forma nella casa d'oggi* exhibition in Como: *Mezzadro* consisted of only a tractor seat mounted onto a frame. The *Sella* stool uses a bicycle saddle as the seat. Numerous furniture, cutlery, and service designs were to follow.

Yet it was with their lighting fixtures, which they designed for Arredoluce, Artemide, and, in particular, for the company Flos, that the brothers were especially successful. Here, too, they focused their efforts on innovative misuse and minimalistic design. Thus a simple streetlamp became the model for the *Arco* floor lamp, and a basic automobile headlight was used as the lamp head for the *Toio* ceiling light. This innovative repurposing of everyday objects and their reuse in the design resulted in the reinvigoration and creative expansion of the concept of "readymade," as invented by Marcel Duchamp in 1912. Many designs for the lighting manufacturer

Flos are today considered to be among the most famous design classics and can also be found in the most important design museums of the world. These include the lights *Taraxcum* (1960), *Splügen Bräu* (1961), *Arco* (1962), the table lamps *Lampadina* (1971) and *Noce* (1972), and the pendant lamp *Frisbi* (1978), which resembles an illuminated UFO. *Brera* (1992) uses the egg as a basic form and has various uses as a wall, floor, table, or ceiling lamp.

In the area of trade fair and exhibition design, Achille Castiglione proved himself to be far ahead of his time. On the occasion of the XI Milan Triennale in 1956, he designed the pavilion for the Italian broadcaster RAI with a spectacular production of construction and lighting elements, text panels, and graphic scaffolding that, in a certain way, anticipated the "deconstructivist" design of later architecture, for example Frank O. Gehry or Zaha Hadid. Subsequent designs of the RAI pavilion were created in the 1960s. Castiglioni also realized important construction projects in the architecture sector, such as the *Torre della PERMANENTE* in Milan (1952–53), the building for the Chamber of Trade and Industry in Milan (1958), the Milan brewery Splügen-Bräu, (1960), the OMEGA office building on the Piazza del Duomo in Milan (1968), and the Castiglioni Haus in Milan (1969). *hd*

1918 Born on February 16 in Milan
1944 Graduates in architecture from the Politecnico di Milano
1947 Start of cooperation with his brothers, Pier Giacomo (1913–1968) and Livio (1911–1979)
1952 His brother Livio leaves the architecture company
1968 Death of his brother Pier Giacomo; Achille continues to run the company alone
1987 Honorary doctorate from the Royal College of Art, London
2001 Honorary doctorate for industrial design from the Politecnico di Milano
2002 Dies in Milan

Portrait of Achille Castiglioni

1902 Alfred Stieglitz founds the
Photo-Secession in New York

1929 Stock market
crash heralds
global economic
crisis

1894 Tower Bridge in London
opened for traffic

1914 Marcel Duchamp's first
readymade, *Bottle Rack*

1850 1855 1860 1865 1870 1875 1880 1885 1890 1895 1900 1905 1910 1915 1920 1925 1930 1935

Vico Magistretti, Maralunga sofa, 1973

1948/49 Berlin Airlift

1982 Michael Jackson, *Thriller*

1992 Founding of the European Union

1939 Germany invades Poland;
World War II commences

1973 Chilean coup d'état; elected president
Salvador Allende dies

| 1940 | 1945 | 1950 | 1955 | 1960 | 1965 | 1970 | 1975 | 1980 | 1985 | 1990 | 1995 | 2000 | 2005 | 2010 | 2015 | 2020 | 2025 |

VICO MAGISTRETTI

Vico Magistretti was one of the founders of elegant Italian style in design. He originally trained as an architect and early on developed the ideal that design should be functional, rational, elegant, and, above all, affordable, too.

Magistretti's designs are characterized by an absence of everything pretentious; his requirement was, in his own words, to design objects that were "anonymous and traditional." They should not come across as conceived, but as having grown from the experience. The fact that he is still relatively unknown outside the design scene, despite the fact that his furniture and lamps sold in millions, also speaks for his pragmatism, the freedom from affectation, and the democratic approach to the products he designed.

Vico Magistretti was born into a Milanese family of architects in 1920, his great-grandfather Gaetano Besia having been a member of the profession. His father, Pier Giulio Magistretti, was involved in the design of the Palazzo dell'Arengario in the Piazza del Duomo.

In 1939, the young Magistretti enrolled in an architecture course at the Politecnico di Milano, but from 1943 on he had to continue in Lausanne in Switzerland in order to avoid deportation to Germany. He soon returned, however, and finally completed his studies in Milan in 1945. At the agency of his father, who had just died and who had worked there his entire life, Magistretti immediately accepted his first commissions with the architect Paolo Chessa. Although he was actually an architect, Magistretti exhibited his self-built pieces of furniture at the R.I.M.A. as early as 1946. He was, however, primarily concerned with town planning tasks and in the 1950s, he designed houses for veterans of the Africa campaign in the QT8 project, a church, and various office buildings.

These early projects and his enormous productivity quickly took Magistretti to the peak of a movement of young architects, and he was regarded as avant-garde, controversial, and modern. At the same time, he began to work with the land surveyor Franco Montella on designs for lamps and pieces of furniture, such as the famous *Carimate* chair. Many simple, highly pragmatic products were created that showed great elegance in both their impression and their design. In his office, Magistretti was still only developing the product ideas, whereas the final construction took place from the end of the 1960s on in close dialogue with manufacturers such as Artemide, Cassina, FontanaArte, Fritz Hansen, Kartell, Knoll, O-Luce, Schiffini, and Campeggi. Magistretti placed great emphasis on considering the production options of his clients so that the designs could be created economically and enable him to remain true to his credo of "design for all."

From his conscientiousness with production matters grew a fascination for plastics in the 1960s. In 1969, he created one of his best-known designs for Artemide, the stackable plastic chair *Selene*, and one year later the stacking chairs *Gaudi* and *Vicario* came to the market. The designs combined traditional forms with the latest production technology and worked sensitively with the constructive and aesthetic possibilities of the material. Even today they are timeless, clever, and stylish.

From the late 1970s on, Magistretti taught at different design schools, including the Royal College of Art in London and the Domus Academy in Milan, although he remained highly productive as an architect and designer. In 1979, he received the Compasso d'Oro, the most important design prize in Italy, for his lamp *Atollo*, and in 1982 he was awarded the Cologne Furniture Fair prize. His *Maui* chair is the top-selling designer chair of all time. A dozen of his designs are exhibited at the Museum of Modern Art in New York, including his *Maralunga* sofa from 1973. He died on September 19, 2006 at the age of 85. *jr*

1920 Vico Magistretti is born in Milan
1939–45 Architecture course at the Politecnico di Milano and in Lausanne
FROM 1945 ON Works in the architecture agency of his deceased father together with Franco Montella
1946 Exhibits at the R.I.M.A., an Italian furniture exhibition
1950s Numerous town planning architectural projects in Milan, including the Torre al Parco (1953–55) and office buildings on the Corso Europa (1955–57)
1960 Works increasingly as an industrial designer
1962 Designs the classic modern chair *Carimate* for Cassina
1969 Designs the plastic chair *Selene* for Artemide
1979 Awarded Compasso d'Oro for his *Atollo* lamp
FROM 1980 ON Professor at the Royal College of Art in London and the Domus Academy in Milan
1997 Awarded the Compasso d'Oro for his life's work
2006 Dies at the age of 85

Portrait of Vico Magistretti

Selene plastic chair, 1969

Maui chair, 1996

1902 Alfred Stieglitz founds the
Photo-Secession in New York

1929 Stock market
crash heralds
global economic
crisis

1894 Tower Bridge in London
opened for traffic

1914 Marcel Duchamp's first
readymade, *Bottle Rack*

| 1850 | 1855 | 1860 | 1865 | 1870 | 1875 | 1880 | 1885 | 1890 | 1895 | 1900 | 1905 | 1910 | 1915 | 1920 | 1925 | 1930 | 1935 |

Michael Graves, 9093 kettle

1939 Germany invades Poland; World War II commences	1965 Joseph Beuys action: "How to explain pictures to a dead hare"	1992 Founding of the European Union
1948/49 Berlin Airlift	1982 Michael Jackson, *Thriller*	2010 "Arab Spring" begins with protests in Tunisia
	1973 Chilean coup d'état; elected president Salvador Allende dies	

1940   1945   1950   1955   1960   1965   1970   1975   1980   1985   1990   1995   2000   2005   2010   2015   2020   2025

ALESSI

Hardly any other manufacturer has influenced the history of household goods to quite the same extent as Alessi. A glance inside museums around the world proves that no other company has so many products in permanent design exhibitions.

Alessi sees itself as an "Italian design factory somewhere between manufacturing and art." Thanks to continual experimental activities, a considerable repertoire of objects has been created over the course of the company's development.

To describe Alessi's style, one must consider Alessi before and after 1970: although the designs were still classically restricted to their function in the early years, in the 1970s, a paradigm switch occurred, triggered by Alberto Alessi and Ettore Sottsass, who changed the old slogan "form follows function" to "family follows function" and thus made Alessi the forerunner of postmodernism.

The origins of the group, which is today known throughout the world, can be traced back to metal processing. At the start, home and desktop devices were manufactured in copper, brass, and nickel silver, later in chrome and silver-plated metal. Although the company was at first heavily influenced by the traditional craftsmanship way of thinking, the son of the founder, Carlo Alessi, succeeded in bringing an important change to the company: he established industrial production and then the use of stainless steel. He also had a greater influence on design. In the 1950s and 1960s, Alessi boosted his reputation with orders for the US army, hotels, and restaurants. The stainless-steel bread-basket, created in 1952, is a symbol of this period. Alessi reduced the design to the basics and limited himself to the pure function. From 1955 on, external designers were commissioned to develop new, fresh ideas. Alessi still works today with freelance designers so that their creativity and freedom is not influenced or restricted by internal company matters. Over the years, Alessi has cooperated with over 500 designers.

Alberto Alessi, who joined the family company in 1970, continued to expand this cooperation. He began with the manufacture of limited and signed ranges created by internationally renowned

designers and architects, and this is what made Alessi known throughout the world.

In addition, it was Alberto Alessi's goal to create good design for all, including for such everyday items as flyswatters and toilet brushes. The costs of the materials also fell. His main aim was to create an emotional relationship between person and object. Products such as Starck's *Juicy Salif* lemon squeezer, the kettle with the bird-shaped whistle by Michael Graves, and Alessandro Mendini's *Anna G.* corkscrew ensured that design now – quite literally – had a face.

Today, there are three brands under which Alessi is sold: The brand "Alessi" represents innovative design and the design classics of the traditional company that are mass produced, "Officina Alessi" is an exclusive brand for individual items and limited series, and the budget brand "A di Alessi" provides high-quality design for the masses. There is also the CSA (Centro Studi Alessi), a center for the development of young designers. Since 1998, objects, proto-types, production machines, drawings, images, and documents of all types can be seen in the Alessi Museum in Crusinallo, on Lake Orta. *nk*

1921 Establishment of FAO (Fratelli Alessi Omegna), a handicrafts workshop run by Giovanni Alessi in Omegna, near Lake Orta, Italy
1935 Son Carlo joins the family company and introduces industrial production
1945 Carlo Alessi becomes managing director; new trademark ALFRA (ALessi FRAtelli); *Bombé* coffee service
1970 Alberto Alessi joins the company; motto: To duplicate art
1982 Starts to produce cutlery with the series *Dry*
1983 Establishment of the subsidiary Officina Alessi for experimental design
1990 Establishment of the CSA (Centro Studi Alessi) for the development of young designers; *Juicy Salif*, lemon squeezer by Philippe Starck
1992 *Pito* kettle by Frank Gehry
1994 *Anna G.* corkscrew by Alessandro Mendini

Richard Sapper, Espresso coffee maker 9090/6M

Basket 370

FC04, Blow up, centerpiece

1893 Edvard Munch, *The Scream*   1917 October Revolution in Russia

1909 Publication of the
Futurist Manifesto

1850 1855 1860 1865 1870 1875 1880 1885 1890 1895 1900 1905 1910 1915 1920 1925 1930 1935

Andrée Putman, Sofa for Ralph Pucci, 2001

TRACEY EMIN

1961 Yuri Gagarin is the first man in space

2001 Terrorist attacks on World Trade Center (9/11)

1949 Founding of the North Atlantic Treaty Organisation

1976 First G7 summit

1996 First cloned mammal (Dolly the sheep)

33 Franklin D. Roosevelt sworn in as president of the US

1954 Premiere of Hitchcock's film *Rear Window*

1987 Black Monday (October 19) sees stock market crash worldwide

2007 iPhone launched

1940 1945 1950 1955 1960 1965 1970 1975 1980 1985 1990 1995 2000 2005 2010 2015 2020 2025

ANDRÉE PUTMAN

Andrée Putman is the "Grande Dame" of French design, a "diva of modern interior design." She gained international recognition for her interior decoration of Morgan's Hotel in New York (1984) with black and white tiles.

These black and white tiles have become her trademark and she has used them in the design of hotel interiors, boutiques, and even the interior of a Concorde. But this is only part of her career, which began in Paris back in the 1950s. Andrée Putman grew up in an upper-class family in St. Germain in Paris, a descendant of the hot-air balloon inventor Montgolfier, and her family property included a Cistercian Abbey in Burgundy, which is a UNESCO World Heritage Site. She was initially destined to be a pianist, but after studying under Francis Poulenc at the Paris Conservatory, she left this discipline and changed her métier. In 1950, she became a fashion and design journalist at the *Femina* newspaper, later also at *Elle*, and then from 1958 to 1967 she was artistic director of the Prisunic chain of department stores. At the Café de Flore, she met contemporary artists, including Pierre Alechinsky, Bram van de Velde, Alberto Giacometti, and Niki de Saint Phalle. In 1978, she founded the successful company Écart, which reproduced furniture and objects from designers of the 1930s, and founded the current company Andrée Putman SARL in 1997.

The modern hotel industry would be inconceivable without the name of Andrée Putman. Her signature style of the black and white tiles at Morgan's Hotel in New York shot her into the international fashion and design scene and she still leaves her mark as a stylish creative director. With her building conversions, interior design, furniture design, and objects, including pieces of jewelry and perfume, she draws on the grand era of the 1920s, when the modern age was still young and Art Deco was an international style. Her greatest period were the frivolous 1980s, when creativity and exhibitionist pleasure were closely linked, when nights were spent dancing at Studio 54 in New York, and when Putman and her company Écart created a furore with designer pieces from the 1930s. The invention of the "boutique hotel," a combination of luxury hotel and shopping mall, marked the start of her ascent into

the world of luxury interior design, which was helped by her sense for refined details and colorful designer furniture. With her instinctive flair for the harmonious coordination of all items of furniture, she has created exquisite interiors for the Saint James Club in Paris, the Wasserturm in Cologne, the Sheraton in Roissy, and the Ritz-Carlton in Wolfsburg, as well as the exterior design of two skyscrapers in Hong Kong (2007), one of which was christened "The Putman." However, the list of carefully selected interior design projects also included private residences and business: the offices for Cartier and Ebel, the office for the former French Minister of Culture, Jack Lang, and the apartments of Karl Lagerfeld, one of her old friends from the "New Design" period, when Ettore Sottsass and Memphis caused a sensation.

In contrast, the style aesthetics of Andrée Putman are almost classical: gray tones, high-quality materials, classic design forms, simple but sophisticated details. She also clarified this with her collection of selected designer pieces; she made the furniture designs of Eileen Gray, Mallet-Stevens, Fortuny, Gaudí, and Lartigue accessible again as reeditions of the design world.

Together with her daughter, Olivia, who joined her company in 2007, Andrée Putman created "French style" in design. She is a master of "good taste," which she continues to defend to this day against all modern innovations. *hd*

1925 Born Andrée Christine Aynard on December 23 in Paris
1943–45 Studies piano under Francis Poulenc at the Conservatoire de Paris
1950 Writes for the fashion magazine *Femina*
1952–58 Design columnist for *Elle*
1958–67 Artistic director of the Prisunic chain of department stores
AT THE END OF THE 1950S Marries the collector and publisher Jacques Putman
1960–64 Interior design editor at *L'œil*
1978 Establishes the Écart design company for interior design
1997 Leaves Écart and sets up the company Andrée Putman SARL
2007 Daughter Olivia takes over management of the company
Andrée Putman lives and works in Paris

Portrait of Andrée Putman

VERNER PANTON

ARNE JACOBSEN

MILES DAVIS

1929 Stock market
crash heralds
global economic
crisis

1911 Wassily Kandinsky,
Impression III

1895 First Venice Biennale

1919 Bauhaus founded by
Walter Gropius in Weimar

1850 1855 1860 1865 1870 1875 1880 1885 1890 1895 1900 1905 1910 1915 1920 1925 1930 1935

Verner Panton, Varna Restaurant Århus, 1971

1950–1953 Korean War

1940–1944 Vichy regime in France

1970 Robert Smithson, *Spiral Jetty*

1961 John F. Kennedy sworn in as president of the US

1993–1997 Frank O. Gehry, Guggenheim Museum, Bilbao

1988 *Freeze*, exhibition of the Young British Artists group in London

2010 Polish president Lech Kaczyński and many other high-ranking Polish officials killed in plane crash

1940 1945 1950 1955 1960 1965 1970 1975 1980 1985 1990 1995 2000 2005 2010 2015 2020 2025

VERNER PANTON

The Panton Chair *by Verner Panton is possibly the most famous chair design of the 20th century. With its futuristic shape and modern materials, it is a symbol for the shift to the colorful plastic and pop world of the 1960s.*

Verner Panton's colorful, sculptural designs make him one of the most innovative designers of the 20th century and also the *enfant terrible* of Danish design. With his furniture, based on geometric shapes, mainly in bright colors, and made out of plastic, he broke with the sleek naturalism of classical Scandinavian design.

Even when he was young, Panton had good connections with the leading Danish designers of his time. At the Royal Danish Academy of Fine Arts, he attended lectures by Poul Henningsen, gained his first employment experience with Arne Jacobsen, and was friends with the teak chair specialist Hans Wegner. And yet he took a completely different path. His passion was for experimentation with plastic and other new materials. The shapes and colors of his designs were inspired by the Op and Pop Art movements of the 1960s and Panton was one of the first in the world to introduce these art forms into the world of architecture and design. He dared to experiment with new materials, shapes, and colors like no other designer.

Panton's almost limitless creativity and his attempts to release himself from preconceived ideas in design are often expressed in his furniture through an absence of traditional elements. Classical chair legs and muted, inconspicuous colors are not to be found in Panton designs. On the contrary, his furniture is based on geometric shapes and has a futuristic-sculptural appearance.

At the start of his career, he created a stir with his innovative architectural ideas, such as the collapsible house (1955), the cardboard house (1957), and the plastic house (1960), before he increasingly devoted himself to interior design in the 1960s. Panton created a number of celebrated pieces of furniture. His first great success was the *Cone Chair*, which he designed in 1959 for his parents' restaurant. The chair, which looks like a floating ice cream cone, caused such a stir at an exhibition in New York that the police had to remove the crowds of people from the shop windows.

His most famous design is the *Panton Chair*, which was named for him. He created his first sketch of a one-piece cantilever chair back in 1955. It was still made from laminate wood but it was his aim to design the first chair created from a single piece of plastic. However, it was almost ten years later, on one of his many trips abroad, that he finally found a manufacturer who dared to work with him on the production of his no-legged chair; this was the Swiss company Vitra. With its smooth, innovative look, the Panton became the chair of its generation.

With his *Living Tower* or *Pantower* and the *Amoebe Highback Chair*, Verner Panton also applied his visions of new, flowing shapes to upholstered furniture. They are mainly used in his legendary room designs, which link together all elements of the room, such as the floor, walls, and ceiling, as well as the furniture, lighting, and textiles, and last but not least the spectacular colors, as an inseparable room unit. *nk*

1926 Born on February 13 in Gamtofte
UNTIL 1951 Studies architecture at the Royal Danish Academy of Fine Arts in Copenhagen
1950–52 Works in the architecture agency of Arne Jacobsen
1955 Establishes his own agency
1963 Moves to Basel, first International Design Award (also 1968 and 1981)
1967 *Panton Chair*
1970 *Living Tower*
1984 Visiting professor of industrial design at the Offenbach Hochschule für Design
1998 Dies in Copenhagen

Portrait of Verner Panton

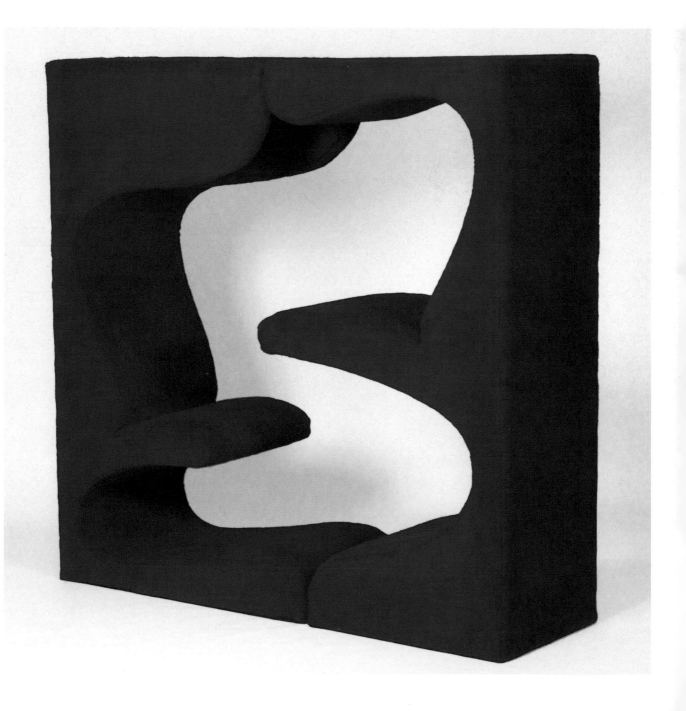

left page
Living Tower, 1968/69

above
Panton chair, c. 1959

1897 Tate Gallery is founded
in London

1919 Founding of the
Weimar Republic

1883 Friedrich Nietzsche publishes
Thus Spoke Zarathustra

1850   1855   1860   1865   1870   1875   1880   1885   1890   1895   1900   1905   1910   1915   1920   1925   1930   1935

Terence Conran, Matador chair, 1990s

DAMIEN HIRST

PIPILOTTI RIST

1939–1945 World War II   1965 Beginning of Vietnam War   1990 German reunification   2010 Volcanic ash from Iceland causes havoc in European airspace

1949 NATO founded   1973 First oil crisis

1958 Truman Capote, *Breakfast at Tiffany's*   1981 First flight by the *Columbia* space shuttle   2002 Euro introduced

1940   1945   1950   1955   1960   1965   1970   1975   1980   1985   1990   1995   2000   2005   2010   2015   2020   2025

TERENCE CONRAN

With his fresh furniture designs, Terence Conran brought modern art to Great Britain. With the motto "Designed to improve the quality of your life ...," the Habitat founder still designs contemporary designer sofas and armchairs to this day.

Sir Terence Conran, who was born in 1931, is one of the best designers in the world. With his chain of Habitat furniture stores, he brought a breath of fresh air to postwar English society. He also set up other companies so that the name Conran became synonymous with new British entrepreneurship. In the 1990s, Conran switched to gastronomy and founded several upmarket restaurants in London, New York, and Paris, and their interior design led the way in terms of style. The company Conran & Partners, which was founded in 1980, provides design services in the fields of architecture, interior design, and town planning.

The creativity of Terence Conran was already apparent in his childhood when he sold homemade toy furniture to his school friends. After studying at the famous Central School of Art and Design, where he became familiar with the Arts and Crafts and Bauhaus movements, Conran's career started when he was just 21 years old as he helped out with furnishings for the Festival of Britain in 1951. Years before the era of "Swinging London," Conran, whose circle of friends included Eduardo Paolozzi and the Independent Group, was an enthusiastic follower of modernity, which was only slowly spreading across England. With his own design company, Conran in 1956 designed his first range of furniture, *Summa*, and a retail outlet for the fashion designer Mary Quant. In 1964, the first Habitat shop opened in the London district of Chelsea. Within a short time, a chain of shops opened across Europe and were very successful at selling functional housewares inspired by Bauhaus products and affordable designer furniture. In 2011, Habitat went bankrupt; most locations in Great Britain faced insolvency proceedings. The 38 branches in Germany, France, and Spain were taken over by the French company Cafom, and the Habitat brand and some branches in London were sold to the British group Home Retail.

After Habitat was founded, other companies were also established in the fields of furniture, fashion,

and decoration. Conran's design company led the way in interior design, product design, and graphic design, as well as in the field of architecture in collaboration with the architect Fred Lloyd Roche.

This profile made Conran one of the leading design specialists in the world and he began at the same time to take an interest in something else: gastronomy. Until then, London, and Great Britain as a whole, had been a gourmet wasteland, and English cooking had had a reputation of being almost inedible. Conran developed a restaurant concept that brought French cooking to England. His restaurants were characterized by a refined combination of stylish interior design and luxury living, often situated in picturesque but dilapidated, archetypal British locations, like Butler's Wharf on the South Bank of the Thames, which was completely renovated and became a flagship for the British Government. To this day, numerous restaurants have been opened across Europe and worldwide, including in Japan. In 2006, the D&D Group run by Conran had a market share of 51 percent of the English gastronomy sector.

Conran's own publisher, Conran Octopus, also published countless books on the "democratization of taste," which Conran pursued, and they were sold throughout the world.

Conran is also heavily committed to design training. Important designers are presented in individual exhibitions in his own Design Museum in Shad Thames, which he founded in 1989. In 2011/12, a major retrospective of his work was held here to celebrate his 80th birthday. *hd*

1931 Born on October 4 in Kingston upon Thames
1948 Starts his textile design studies at the Central School of Art and Design
1952 Establishes Conran & Company with his own furniture designs
1953 First Soup Kitchen opens in London based on French model; introduction of espresso machines (Gaggia)
1956 Establishes the Conran Design Group; interior design for Mary Quant
1964 Creates the Habitat shops
1980 Establishes the Conran Foundation with the aim of promoting new British industrial design
1983 Receives a knighthood
1989 Design Museum London opens in Butler's Wharf
1991 Establishes the restaurant group Conran Restaurants
2004 Awarded the Prince Philip Designer's Prize
2007 Receives honorary doctorate from South Bank University, London
2011/12 Retrospective of his work at the Design Museum London

Portrait of Terence Conran

above
Toaster for Tchibo (from the kitchen
range for Tchibo with Sebastian Conran),
2007

right page
Hector Bibendum blue cord table lamp,
2011

1888 Vincent van Gogh, *The Night Café*

1916 Albert Einstein,
Theory of Relativity

1929 The Museum of
Modern Art
opens in New
York

1905 German Expressionist group
Die Brücke is founded in Dresden

1850　1855　1860　1865　1870　1875　1880　1885　1890　1895　1900　1905　1910　1915　1920　1925　1930　1935

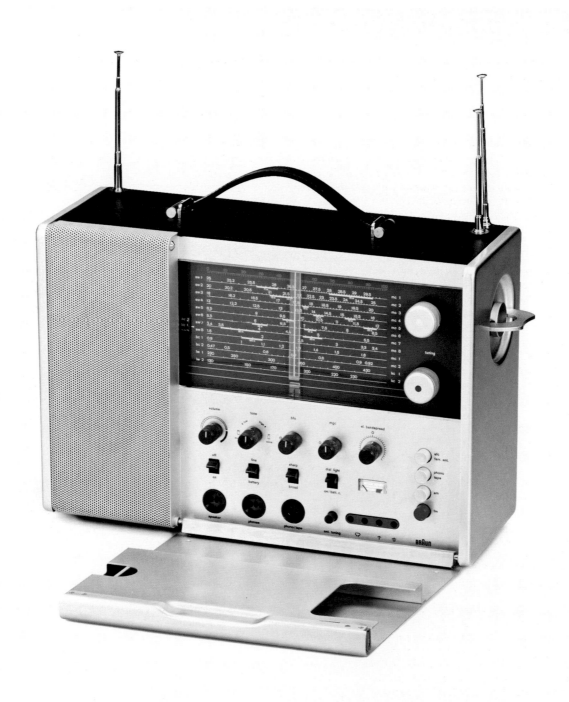

JONATHAN IVE

1945 Atom bombs dropped on
Hiroshima and Nagasaki
1961 Founding of Amnesty International
1989 Fall of the Berlin Wall
2006 A tsunami kills more than
500 people on Java
1949 Founding of the German
Democratic Republic
1995 Christo and Jeanne-Claude
veil the Reichstag in Berlin
1933 Adolf Hitler comes
to power
1971 First Starbucks opens
1955 Beginning of Pop Art

1940 1945 1950 1955 1960 1965 1970 1975 1980 1985 1990 1995 2000 2005 2010 2015 2020 2025

DIETER RAMS

"Good design is innovative, aesthetic, unobtrusive, honest, long-lasting, thorough down to the last detail, environmentally friendly, and is self-explanatory."

For 60 years, Dieter Rams has been transferring his ideas of simplicity and clarity to iconic products. His designs for the Braun and Vitsœ companies in the second half of the 20th century demonstrate the perfect composition of technology, aesthetics, and communication in exemplary elegance. The awards he has received and the influence of his design philosophy on product and furniture design make him one of the most important designers of our time. He formulated his own credo with the "Ten Principles for Good Design": they are quasi-ethical principles that elevate design above the simple styling so frequently practiced today and give it a purpose and justification. They have lost none of their validity and are still important guidelines for contemporary young designers, even with the move toward sustainable consumption.

Rams was born in Wiesbaden in 1932 and was introduced to the design and manufacture of utility objects at an early age by his grandfather, who was a carpenter. In 1947, at the age of 15, he began to study architecture, although he interrupted this course from 1948 to 1951 to train as a carpenter. In 1953, he finally graduated as an architect and got his first job at the agency of Otto Apel. In 1955, he moved to the electronic appliance manufacturer Braun AG, where he first worked as an interior designer for offices and exhibition stands. However, he soon became interested in products and their development and, with his rational approach, he began to have a significant influence on Braun's product design.

In 1956, Rams and Hans Gugelot from the Ulm School designed a product that today represents his work like no other: the *Braun SK 4* combined radio and record player. The device had a white-painted cuboid body made of metal, which was very unusual for "audio furniture" at that time (Hans Gugelot), and also a cover made of acrylic glass that gave it the nickname "Snow White's coffin." The arrangement of the fittings on the upper side of the device

was a change to the paradigm and characterized Braun products from then on. In the mid-1960s, Rams perfected the design, in particular the structure and interfaces, so that all audio devices manufactured by the company had the same dimensions and could thus be combined vertically or horizontally. This system concept and the disclosure of technical functions now represented an expression of modernity and fitted perfectly with the progressive focus of the time.

The rational materialism, reduced design, and the clear graphical structure with high product and production quality evolved into a trademark for Braun AG, where Rams became manager of the design department in 1961 and director of product design. The designs created under his direction are so consistent and so minimal that the introduction of the additional color of black at the start of the 1980s was considered by the customers to be almost too radical. Before Rams left the company in 1997, he created products such as the *Multimix MX 32* (1958), the *T 1000* multiband radio (1962), the *Sixtand S* shaver (1968), the *HLD 1000* hairdryer, and the *Domo Quartz ABW 21* wall clock (1979). Since the turn of the century, his achievements have received increased recognition as Jonathan Ive, head of design at Apple, was inspired by Ram's designs for the design of the iPod and other Apple products.

With all his clarity and lack of comprise, Dieter Rams has never become a missionary of his principles. Ettore Sottsass, one of the "Memphis" movement diametrically opposed to Rams, said of him: "Dieter was so good at [...] not tormenting himself and others that his design ultimately appeared clear, calm, always accepted, understandable, and self-explanatory." *jr*

1932 Born on May 20 in Wiesbaden
1943–53 Studies architecture and carpentry at the Werkkunstschule Wiesbaden
1953–55 Works at the architecture agency of Otto Apel
FROM 1955 ON Architect and interior designer for Braun
1956 Designs the *Braun SK 4* together with Hans Gugelot
FROM 1957 ON Furniture designer for Otto Zapf (today sdr+)
1961–95 Head of design at Braun
1964 Exhibition at documenta III in Kassel
1965 Berlin Art Prize
1981 Professor of industrial design at the HFBK Hamburg
2002 Highest Order of Merit from the Federal Republic of Germany
2007 Lucky Strike Designer Award for his life's work

left page
Dieter Rams, T 1000 multiband radio, 1962

above
Portrait of Dieter Rams

1891 Construction of Trans-Siberian
Railway begins

1913 Armory Show in New York shows
the European avant-garde

1901 Queen Victoria dies

1906 San Francisco earthquake

1928 Alexander Fleming
discovers penicillin

1850 1855 1860 1865 1870 1875 1880 1885 1890 1895 1900 1905 1910 1915 1920 1925 1930 1935

1965 First Op Art exhibition,
The Responsive Eye in New York

1939–1945 World War II

1976 Apple Computers founded

1959 Completion of the Solomon
R. Guggenheim Museum in New York

1999 First e-book reader

2006 Jackson Pollock's *No. 5*
sold for \$140m

1992 Maastricht Treaty establishes the EU

1940   1945   1950   1955   1960   1965   1970   1975   1980   1985   1990   1995   2000   2005   2010   2015   2020   2025

INGO MAURER

From the lighting systems for the Atomium in Brussels to the original Mozzkito tea strainer table lamp, Ingo Maurer plays with lights in all its facets. His lights are technically complex, imaginatively designed, and often seasoned with a pinch of humor or irony.

Ingo Maurer's medium is light, his muse is the lightbulb. Fascinated by the archetype of the naked lightbulb and inspired by Pop Art, which he came across in the US at the start of the 1960s, he created his first lamp design in 1966: *Bulb* – an oversized lightbulb of handblown glass illuminated by a real lightbulb. The ingenious idea of making the light source into the lamp itself, and thus creating an ironic interplay between the form and function, shot Maurer to stardom.

In Maurer's eyes, the naked lightbulb represents a perfect symbiosis of industry and poetic expression. "The light of a lightbulb is heat and fire," according to Maurer. And so it appeared again and again in his work over the following decades, be it winged with goose feathers (*Lucellino*, 1992), or virtually as a hologram on a lampshade (*Wo bist du, Edison?*, 1997). More recently, a heat-resistant silicon cover that turns a clear lightbulb into a frosted one (*Euro-Condom*, 2009) and an empty lightbulb without a tungsten filament (*WoonderLux*, 2010) show Maurer's creative reaction to the European ban on lightbulbs.

Maurer was such an advocate of the good old lightbulb that with *WoonderLux* he combines the classic form of the lightbulb with modern LED light technology hidden in the base to illuminate the lamp. He was one of the first to experiment with halogen at the start of the 1980s, and in 1984, he first presented the first of his halogen light systems, *YaYaHo*, in which low-voltage cables were strung in a room with small halogen lamps that can be arranged individually. Together with Osram, he developed the first lamp to use energy-efficient organic light diodes, or OLEDs, (*Early Future* table lamp, 2008).

Maurer is also fascinated by paper as a material. In one of his most famous designs, the *Zettel'z* light (1998), 49 small pieces of Japanese paper are fixed around the light source on wires like rays. The papers are printed with poetry texts or drawings,

while blank pieces invite further creative decoration. Maurer had already designed a lighting group with fans made out of bamboo and rice paper (*Uchiwa*) in 1973. He plays with the creative options of the material, pleats it, creases it (*Knitterling* pendulum light), or silver-plates it (*Oh Mei Ma*).

In recent years, the innovative lamp designer has followed new paths and created a stir with his imaginative light installations and lighting concepts for buildings and open areas. In 1999, for example, he bathed the Munich subway station Westfriedhof in a warm light with eleven enormous, shell-like, aluminum lampshades. The *Domes* look like oversized heat lamps with a diameter of almost four meters and were subsequently mass-produced in a smaller variant as *XXL Domes*. Ten years later, when the Münchner Freiheit station was redesigned, Maurer used a mirrored roof lit by over 200 square light boxes to invigorate the space with light animations in blue and yellow. *ch*

1932 Born on the island of Reichenau, Lake Constance
1954–58 After training as a typesetter, he studies graphic design in Munich
1960–63 Works as a graphic designer and designer in San Francisco and New York
1966 Sets up the company Design M for lamps and lighting concepts; first light design *Bulb*
1984 *YaYaHo*, the first low-voltage lighting system with 276 individual parts
1992 *Lucellino*
1994 Pendant light *Porca Miseria!* with shattered crockery
1998 Illuminates the platform and Park & Ride area at the underground station Westfriedhof, Munich
2006 Lighting objects and lighting systems for the Atomium, Brussels
2008 Develops an OLED lamp with Osram
2010 Awarded the Design Prize of the Federal Republic of Germany for his life's work

left page
Ingo Maurer, Westfriedhof subway station, Munich, 1998

above
Portrait of Ingo Maurer

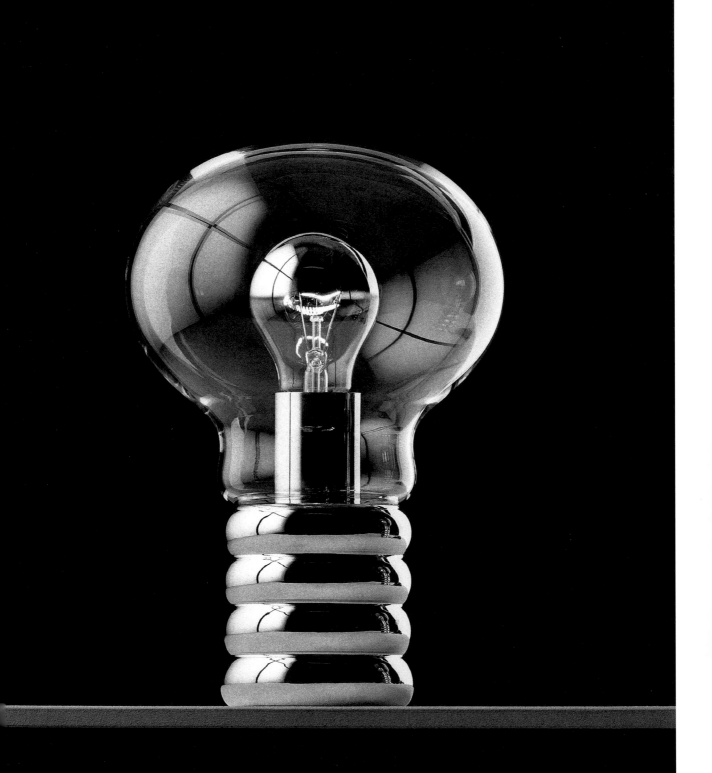

left page
Bulb

above
Lucellino

1900 Boxer Rebellion in China

1914 Assassination of Archduke Franz Ferdinand of Austria on June 28; World War I breaks out

1929 Stock market crash heralds global economic crisis

1850   1855   1860   1865   1870   1875   1880   1885   1890   1895   1900   1905   1910   1915   1920   1925   1930   1935

Philippe Starck, Lou Read Chair, 2011

1940	1945	1950	1955	1960	1965	1970	1975	1980	1985	1990	1995	2000	2005	2010	2015	2020	2025	

PHILIPPE STARCK

With his sensual, attractive, and often crazy designs, the rock star of the design world became one of the best-known interior and industrial designers of all time. As a leading representative of New Design, the Frenchman liked to surprise and shock and was even happy to step into the spotlight himself.

From chairs, lights, baths, and candlesticks to motorbikes and yachts to kitchen utensils, groceries, and a flyswatter – anyone wishing to do so could surround himself with objects by Philippe Starck. Those who enter the world of Starck's design find happiness, fantasy, modern rationality, a pinch of irony, and always surprises. But those looking for a consistent style will be disappointed. Starck casually combines different style periods, directions, materials, and production techniques – what Philippe Starck designs is just Starck. He is unrivaled in his ability to sense and satisfy the spirit of the moment. When the trend toward increased emotionality and less functionality prevailed in the 1980s and 1990s, he designed objects that also created associations with their offbeat names.

Starck's career began very early: when he was just 16 years old, he won the La Vilette furniture competition with his inflatable seats, and by the age of 20 he was artistic director for the fashion designer Pierre Cardin. He then devoted himself to interior design and furnished the La Main Bleue bar in Montreuil and the Les Bains Douches club in Paris, for example. His career was boosted by a commission from François Mitterrand, who entrusted him and four other interior designers with the design of his private rooms in the Élysée Palace in 1982. Two years later, the opening of the Café Costes in Paris, for which Starck designed all furnishings, created an international sensation. The three-legged *Costes* chair became an international sales hit with its tubular steel feet, curved wood back of mahogany laminate, and leather upholstery. These two projects raised him to the status of an internationally celebrated star designer. In particular, his collaboration with such renowned manufacturers as Alessi, Flos, Vitra, Baccarat, and Samsonite, and the grandiose design of exclusive hotels, restaurants, and boutiques such as the Royalton in New York and the Delano in Miami and of boutiques for Jean-Paul Gaultier, Hugo Boss, and Yamamoto secured his fame.

Starck's pieces are characterized by their names, which are always humorous and which lend a unique character to the furniture and product designs. The *Richard III* chair, for example, is a bulky and powerful design while the *Lola Mundo* chair is feminine and delicate with its filigree, curving legs.

His most financially profitable designs include the *Ara* table lamp (1988), the *Juicy Salif* lemon squeezer (1990), the *Max le Chinois* sieve (1990), and the *Hot Bertaa* kettle (1990). With the *Louis Ghost* chair (2002), he succeeded in creating a successful and also technically highly demanding design as the complete chair consists of only a single element manufactured in an injection-molding process. This was a true New Design object that illustrated the dematerialization of design. *nk*

left
Mama Shelter Marseilles, 2012

above
Portrait of Philippe Starck

1917 October Revolution
in Russia

1909 Publication of the
Futurist Manifesto

| 1850 | 1855 | 1860 | 1865 | 1870 | 1875 | 1880 | 1885 | 1890 | 1895 | 1900 | 1905 | 1910 | 1915 | 1920 | 1925 | 1930 | 1935 |

Verner Panton, Amoebe Chair, 1970

TADAO ANDŌ

933 Franklin D. Roosevelt sworn in as president of the US

1954 Premiere of Hitchcock's film *Rear Window*

1961 Yuri Gagarin is the first man in space

1949 Founding of the North Atlantic Treaty Organisation

1976 First G7 summit

1987 Black Monday (October 19) sees stock market crash worldwide

2001 Terrorist attacks on World Trade Center (9/11)

1996 First cloned mammal (Dolly the sheep)

1940 1945 1950 1955 1960 1965 1970 1975 1980 1985 1990 1995 2000 2005 2010 2015 2020 2025

VITRA

What would good design be without the right manufacturer? The Swiss furniture manufacturer Vitra has set itself the goal of optimizing collaboration between designer and manufacturer in order to develop exclusive, long-lasting, high-quality, and inspiring products.

From Charles and Ray Eames to Verner Panton, Ettore Sottsass, and Jean Prouvé to Frank Gehry, Philippe Starck, and Jasper Morrison – the list of Vitra's collaborative partners reads like a Who's Who of the international design elite. In addition to the reissue of design classics and the development of avant-garde pieces of furniture, the manufacturer's efforts to encourage exhibition management and the expansion of the production location into an architecture park have also long since turned Vitra into a design institution. Vitra also sees itself as being not only a manufacturer, but rather as a project with the aim of redesigning the world.

The company was founded in 1950 when Willi Fehlbaum set up the company Vitra in Weil am Rhein with his wife, Erika. Fehlbaum achieved a significant coup in 1957 when, during a trip to the US, he acquired the licenses to produce the Herman Miller Collection for Europe. This included all designs by the design duo Charles and Ray Eames and by George Nelson. When Vitra developed and produced the *Panton Chair* in 1967 with Verner Panton, the company again demonstrated its sense for unusual furniture designs. In the 1970s, the company concentrated on the combination of ergonomics and good design, a new concept at the time, and manufactured very successful office furniture. In 1981, the factory was almost destroyed in a major fire.

The son, Rolf Fehlmann, who had managed Vitra since 1977, decided to completely redesign the production location and laid the foundation for the current Vitra Campus. Over time, it became a "design destination" that attracted numerous famous architects and designers. In addition to the production buildings designed by Nicholas Grimshaw, the Design Museum was constructed in 1989 by Frank O. Gehry and today it is one of the leading design museums in the world. It has a collection of over 6,000 pieces of furniture, 2,000 lights, and 3,000 designs and construction plans

from well-known designers and manufacturers from 1850 to today. In 1993, Zaha Hadid, still unknown at the time, designed the spectacular, futuristic fire station for the site, followed by a garage designed by Jean Prouvé, a production hall by Álvaro Siza Vieira, and a conference pavilion by Tadao Ando – and finally, the newest development, in 2010, was the VitraHaus by Herzog & de Meuron. It holds the Vitra Home Collection and provides inspiration for interior design in twelve nested, gable-roofed houses. The visitor can select a preferred variant of the Eames classic in the Lounge Chair Atelier and observe how the unique piece is made by hand.

Vitra has supported and promoted international avant-garde furniture since the 1970s. The Vitra Edition, in particular, enables designers to create experimental items in a limited edition with market or production-related restrictions. Together with their extensive collection of important furniture designs and the research and exhibition projects, Vitra has had a constant influence on contemporary design. *nk*

1950 Founding of the Vitra company in Weil am Rhein
1957 Willi Fehlbaum receives the sales license for the Miller Collection for Europe
1977 Rolf Fehlbaum takes over Vitra, his brother Raymond the Fehlbaum shop-fitting business
1981 Major fire in Weil am Rhein, redesign by Nicholas Grimshaw
1987 Introduction of the Vitra Edition
1989 Opening of the Vitra Design Museum
2000 Opening of the Vitra Design Museum branch in Berlin
2002 Introduction of the Vitra Home Collection
2010 Opening of the VitraHaus

Mario Bellini, Figura II, 1984

Charles and Ray Eames,
Lounge Chair, 1956

1911 Ernest Rutherford develops
his model of the atom

1902 Alfred Stieglitz's *Camera Work*
is founded

1925 Invention of television

1850 1855 1860 1865 1870 1875 1880 1885 1890 1895 1900 1905 1910 1915 1920 1925 1930 1935

left
Ron Arad, Well Tempered Chair, 1986

below
Design Museum in Holon, Israel, 2010

1940 McDonald's is founded

1962 Cuban Missile Crisis

1989 Portable Game Boy console launched

1970 British rock band Queen form

1997 Death of Princess Diana

1955 *The Family of Man* exhibition at MoMA in New York

1977 German Autumn (Baader-Meinhof gang)

2004 EU expands eastward

| 1940 | 1945 | 1950 | 1955 | 1960 | 1965 | 1970 | 1975 | 1980 | 1985 | 1990 | 1995 | 2000 | 2005 | 2010 | 2015 | 2020 | 2025 |

RON ARAD

With an unbelievable feeling for uniqueness, Ron Arad has designed objects ranging from a stereo set to chairs to architecture.

In his designs, Ron Arad rarely looks for the pragmatic option. Instead, he consciously also sees design as an artistic expression. Maybe it is because of this that he has also been very commercially successful over the past 30 years. His ideas are sometimes controversial and, during the early years in particular, they often flirted with the confines of fine art, albeit strong conceptual art. Nevertheless, his work can hardly be seen as a social commentary; to awaken desire in the observer is always part of the commission for this all-rounder.

Ron Arad was born the son of a painter and an architect in Tel Aviv in 1951. Like so many Israeli designers, his artistic career began at the Bezalel Academy of Arts and Design. However, he did not stay there long. In 1973, he moved to the avant-garde Architectural Association School of Architecture in London, where he was taught by Peter Cook, a founder of the Archigram movement. Arad's fellow students included Zaha Hadid and Nigel Coates, and he finally completed his studies in 1979.

In 1981, he and Caroline Thorman set up their own studio, called One Off, which was both a workshop and a showroom for his designs. Here, Arad initially produced unique items with simple materials. The studio was not just the birthplace of his own experimental creations but was also a contact point for other conceptual designers such as Tom Dixon, Danny Lane, and Tom Lynham, who exhibited their work here. From this environment emerged the *Rover Chair* in 1981, which was created from an automobile seat, and *Concrete Stereo*, which was an audio system molded from concrete. In 1986, Arad received his first commission for Vitra, for whom he designed what has since become the legendary *Well Tempered Chair*. This construction of steel sheets and winged screws plays with visual conventions and is still one of his best-known pieces. In 1987, the *Sticks and Stones* exhibition was launched for the ten-year anniversary of the Centre Pompidou in Paris. Arad pressed chairs provided by visitors into cuboid blocks using a specially designed machine and then built a wall with them. During the same year, he also exhibited the *Carpet Chair* and the *Curtain Call* installation at documenta VIII in Kassel.

In 1988, Ron Arad won the tender to design the reception area for the Tel Aviv Opera House. To manage the extensive planning tasks and to meet the growing demand for his products, Arad founded the design agency Ron Arad Associates Ltd in 1989. From this platform he developed the *Bookworm* in 1994 for the Milan company Kartell, which became his greatest commercial success to date. The bookshelves, which were manufactured from flexible but stable plastic, can be installed by customers as required and link unconventional design with perfect mastery of the material while being simultaneously used in various ways.

This virtuosity when dealing with the different disciplines of design still distinguishes Ron Arad today. His curving Cor-Ten steel architecture, which often appears impossible, the combination of technical knowledge with daring material combinations, and his unerring instinct for the spirit of the times make Ron Arad one of the most important and influential designers of our time. One Off and Ron Arad Associates are still involved with product design and architectural projects today. The studios regularly work for customers such as Alessi, Kartell, Moroso, Driade, and Magis. *jr*

1951 Ron Arad is born in Tel Aviv, Israel

1971 Studies at the Bezalel Academy of Arts and Design in Jerusalem

1973 Moves to the Architectural Association School of Architecture in London, graduating in 1979

1981 Establishes the One Off agency and showroom with Caroline Thorman

1986 Designs the *Well Tempered Chair*

1987 *Sticks and Stones* exhibition at the Centre Pompidou in Paris

1988 Winning design with C. Norton and S. McAdam for the design of the foyer and reception area of the Opera House in Tel Aviv

1989 Sets up Ron Arad Associates Ltd with Alison Brooks

1994 Presentation of *Bookworm*

1997–2009 Professor at the Royal College of Art in London, first for furniture design, later for product design

2010 Opens the first design museum in Israel in Holon, which Arad had planned with Bruno Asa

Portrait of Ron Arad

1850 1855 1860 1865 1870 1875 1880 1885 1890 1895 1900 1905 1910 1915 1920 1925 1930 1935

left
Tom Dixon, Fin Light, 2012

above
Copper Shade, 2005

1993 Bombay bombings   **2007** Al Gore awarded Nobel Peace Prize

1960 Clement Greenberg,   **1973** US Supreme Court   **1986** First modular space   **2010** "Arab Spring" begins with
Modernist Painting   legalizes abortion   station Mir; Challenger   protests in Tunisia

1940 Trotsky murdered in Mexico   **1964** Racial segregation abolished in the US   space shuttle disaster   **2001** Apple iPod launched

1940   1945   1950   1955   1960   1965   1970   1975   1980   1985   1990   1995   2000   2005   2010   2015   2020   2025

TOM DIXON

As diverse as the designs by Tom Dixon may appear, they are invariably blunt, inspired by different periods, sprinkled with British punk glamor, and always robust.

Even without formal training, Tom Dixon is today considered one of the most significant contemporary British designers alongside Ron Arad and James Dyson. His most famous designs include the *Mirror Ball* and *Copper Shade* lamps, along with the *S Chair* and the plastic lamp *Jack*. Dixon's contemporary glamorous style is inspired in equal measure by design classics and by new materials and production technologies. He appeals to both young and old and, thanks to different lines and manufacturers, also to the mass market as well as the top market segment.

When he left the Chelsea School of Art after just six months, Tom Dixon was part of a group of young British designers who, inspired by the punk movement, began to work with welded metal in the 1980s. Under the name "creative salvage," the group achieved recognition, although it was limited to eccentric one-off pieces and limited editions. The *Kitchen* chair (1987) is typical for this phase and integrates "objets trouvés" such as frying pans and soup ladles.

At the start of the 1990s, Dixon turned more toward the commercialization of his designs. He founded the studio Space, where he designed more than 50 models of the sculptural *S Chair*. It consists of curved steel and is covered with different materials. In 1987, the Italian furniture manufacturer Giulio Cappellini discovered the *S Chair* and took it to mass production.

In 1998, Dixon was offered the position of head designer at Habitat and later described this period as "his first proper job." Here, the self-taught designer could extend his creativity and industrial knowledge to the fields of mass production, production processes, and cost calculations. At the same time, he subjected the rather dusty label to modernization. In particular, the reissue of design classics and the promotion of aspiring designers at Habitat can be attributed to Tom Dixon.

In 2002, he founded Tom Dixon. The Company. Two years later he joined the furniture manufacturer Artek, which had been set up 70 years earlier by the Finn Alvar Aalto. Since then, his aim has been to bring new life to the British furniture industry with solid designs on the one hand and innovations on the other. In accordance with this principle, he designed the *Fresh Fat* series, for which he knotted and wove plastic string so that he could create vessels and even chairs and tables that looked as if they were made of glass. In 2003, he experimented with tableware and designed the *eco ware* series, which consisted of 85 percent bamboo fibers and biodegradable plastic. In 2005, he created the very elegant series of lamps *Copper Shade* and *Mirror Ball*, which were created from reflective plastic but look like shining metal.

In addition to designs for his own company, Dixon also cooperated with famous companies such as Veuve Clicquot, Swarovski, and Terence Conran, as well as with such personalities as Vivienne Westwood and Jean Paul Gaultier. In spite of his avant-garde reputation, Dixon has always followed his very democratic objectives: to promote young talent and to produce good design for everyone. *nk*

1959 Born in Sfax, Tunisia
1978 Expulsion from Chelsea School of Art, London
1987 Dixon PID, later Space, own studio and factory
1991 S Chair (Cappellini)
1996 Eurolounge
1997 Millennium Mark Award
1998 Head of design at Habitat
2000 Order of the British Empire (OBE) for services to design
2002 Establishes Tom Dixon. The Company
2004 Honorary doctorate from Birmingham City University
2004 Creative director at Artek

Portrait of Tom Dixon

1850　1855　1860　1865　1870　1875　1880　1885　1890　1895　1900　1905　1910　1915　1920　1925　1930　1935

1945 Marilyn Monroe discovered
as photographic model

1966 Barnett Newman, *Who's Afraid
of Red, Yellow and Blue*

1985 Live Aid concert
for Africa

2001 First same-sex "marriage"
in Holland

1939–1945 World War II

1957 Ghana is first African colony to gain
independence after World War II

1975 Pol Pot comes to power
in Cambodia

1995 *Toy Story* is first movie
produced entirely with
computer animation

2008 Summer Olympics in
Beijing, China

1940   1945   1950   1955   1960   1965   1970   1975   1980   1985   1990   1995   2000   2005   2010   2015   2020   2025

JASPER MORRISON

The Briton is one of the most influential contemporary product and furniture designers. With his simple, stripped-back design, he is considered a representative of "New Simplicity."

In 2006, Morrison and the Japanese designer Naoto Fukasawa curated the exhibition *Super Normal*. On display was a selection of 204 everyday objects, including those with an anonymous design, such as a potato peeler, plastic trash can, and paper clips, as well as design classics such as the 606 *Shelving System* by Dieter Rams for Vitsoe, the *Tulip Chair* by Eero Saarinen for Knoll, and contemporary designs, for example the futuristic office system *Joyn* by Ronan and Erwan Bouroullec. The exhibition was an homage to straightforward design and to the beauty of simple, intelligently made everyday objects.

The work by Morrison can also be described as "supernormal." For him, functionality is key for the quality of a product, not design. His own designs are characterized by the simplicity of their construction and a highly minimalist use of forms.

Jaspar Morrison achieved his first major success as a furniture designer with the *Ply Chair* (1989) for Vitra, created out of nothing but plywood, glue, and screws. He had originally designed the chair for the *Some New Items for the Home* exhibition in Berlin (1988) – a minimalist room installation made entirely from plywood, which signified a return to reduced design and also a reaction to the postmodernist formal excesses of the 1980s. Rolf Fehlbaum, chairman of Vitra, noticed the young designer and included his chair in his program.

"The main reason why Ply-Chair looks the way it does today is that I had to make it myself and the only tools available to me were an electric compass saw and a number of pieces of wood," explains Morrison.

Morrison's breakthrough as a product designer came in 1990 with the design of the *Series 1144* door handles for FSB. In its reduced form, the door handle appears unobtrusive, but like a tool, it is perfectly adapted to the anatomy of the hand. The series won him Germany's Bundespreis Produkt Design award and the iF Top Ten Award. "You shouldn't have to think about how to use a door handle," he says, explaining his approach to design, which becomes consciously tangible not so much through the product's appearance as through the way it is used.

In subsequent years, Morrison established himself as an all-around designer with numerous designs for internationally renowned companies such as Alessi, Cappellini, Magis, Flos, Rowenta, Vitra, and Olivetti. The extensive body of works by this British minimalist includes furniture – with 22 different chair models alone – as well as lamps, crockery, household goods, sanitary items, household and electronic devices, home accessories, and textiles. In addition, together with his design agency, he has also designed various exhibitions (including *Danish Design – I like it!* in 2011, for the Designmuseum Danmark) and has developed projects in the area of urban design, for example a bus stop for the Vitra company in 2006. *aw*

1959 Born in London, England
1979–85 Studies at the Kingston Polytechnic Design School and at the Royal College of Art in London
1984 Scholarship to the Hochschule der Künste, Berlin
1986 Establishes his first agency, Design Jasper Morrison Limited, in London
1987 Participates in documenta VIII in Kassel with the installation *Reuters News Centre*
1988 *Some New Items for the Home*, installation at the DAAD Galerie, Berlin
1995 Wins the competition to design the new tram for Hanover
1999 Solo exhibition at the Axis Gallery, Tokyo
2002 Monograph *Everything But The Walls*
2003 Opens his second agency, in Paris
2006 First *Super Normal* exhibition, in Tokyo
2009 Opens the Jasper Morrison Limited Shop in London

left page
Jasper Morrison, Glo-Ball, 1999

above
Portrait of Jasper Morrison, 2007

ETTORE SOTTSASS

VICTOR VASARELY

1933 Franklin
D. Roosevelt
sworn in as
1917 October Revolution   president of
in Russia   the US

1850   1855   1860   1865   1870   1875   1880   1885   1890   1895   1900   1905   1910   1915   1920   1925   1930   1935

1940 1945 1950 1955 1960 1965 1970 1975 1980 1985 1990 1995 2000 2005 2010 2015 2020 2025

KARIM RASHID

The internationally renowned designer Karim Rashid wanted to change the world with his soft, colored shapes, and became a pop star of the design world with his "blobism."

Karim Rashid is one of the most productive designers of his generation. He has created over 3,000 designs for numerous famous companies such as Artemide, Cappellini, Magis, LaCie, Samsung, Veuve Cliquot, and Swarowski, and has won more than 300 international design prizes, such as the Good Design Award (South Africa), the Good Design Award (Japan), the red dot design award, and the Design Plus Award. His most popular products include the *Garbo Can* trash basket and the *Oh Chair* plastic chair. Rashid's interior designs for the Morimoto Restaurant in Philadelphia and the Semiramis Hotel in Athens also won prizes, as did exhibitions for Deutsche Bank and Audi. His works can be found in the collections of renowned museums such as the Museum of Modern Art in New York.

Karim Rashid is the pop star of the design world. Even the outfits worn by the designer, who was born in Cairo and grew up in Canada, live up to every common cliché that the layman could have of this profession: wearing large, horn-rimmed glasses, a white suit, and sneakers, this industrial designer, who works in New York, designs everything from trash cans to fashion accessories, from furniture and electronic products to trendy interiors for hotels and restaurants such as the Semiramis Hotel in Athens, the Morimoto Restaurant in Philadelphia, and the Powder Club in New York. He can also be regularly found enjoying the nightlife of Manhattan as "DJ Electronikreemy." He is not, however, an inventor of new, never-before-seen designs, nor is he a super-star of design like Marc Newson or Philippe Starck. Rashid has simple, popular taste that captures the spirit of the time and appeals to trend-conscious youth in particular. Just as a music studio remixes old songs with digital technology and samples different music styles, Rashid plays and composes with the style elements of modern design and then converts them into his own signature style. The internationally recognized design star focuses on the sense of color he has derived from Pop Art, and

on the psychedelic patterns of the 1960s and other references from the history of design and modern art – from the Op Art of Vasarely to the memorable patterns of the graffiti scene.

After graduating in industrial design from Carleton University in Ottawa in 1982, Rashid completed further design studies under Ettore Sottsass in Naples and Rodolfo Bonetto in Milan. In 1993, he opened his own design studio in New York and soon made a name for himself with his designs, whose gaudy colors and round forms became sensual references to the pop period of the 1960s and 1970s. Rashid celebrated his international breakthrough in 1996 with the plastic trash basket *Garbo Can*. Since then, he has designed over 3,000 objects and received over 300 design prizes. The modernist references of his design products include the design heroes of the past, whom he likes to specify himself:

"Ettore Sottsass, Gaetano Pesce, Rodolfo Bonetto, Ron Arad, Philippe Starck, Luigi Colani, Joe Colombo, Charles Eames, and so many others … "

Rashid is not squeamish about dealing with his famous predecessors. For example, he used Autocad to morph Charles Eames's *Chaise* into jaunty, stackable discount chairs. The main point is that everything is round, sweeping, without corners and edges, and as bright as possible, for example turquoise and pink, apparently his favorite colors. Rashid describes his own style as "sensual minimalism" or simply as "blobism," which would be a sad phenomenon were it not for Rashid's sense of humor. And the sales figures for his products, which are sold by well-known companies, speak for themselves: 2.5 million units of his vacuum cleaner have been sold, as well as millions of trash baskets and other fashion articles ranging from a perfume bottle to the total concept (corporate identity) for a design exhibition and a subway station in Naples (2011).

Karim Rashid also has the gift of being able to design mass articles for a mass market and sell them. *hd*

1960 Born on September 18 in Cairo
1982 Bachelor degree in industrial design at the Carleton University of Ottawa
1993 Own design studio in New York
1996 International breakthrough with the *Garbo Can*
2001 Monograph *I Want to Change the World*
2005/06 Honorary Doctorate from the Corcoran College of Art and Design, Washington, D.C., and the Ontario College of Art & Design, Toronto
2008 Marries the Serbian chemist Ivana Puric
Karim Rashid lives and works in New York and Rotterdam.

left page
Morph, One-Dress for One, 2000

above
Portrait of Karim Rashid

next double page
University of Naples subway station, Naples, 2011

1930 Grant Wood,
American Gothic

1919 Treaty of Versailles officially
ends World War I

| 1850 | 1855 | 1860 | 1865 | 1870 | 1875 | 1880 | 1885 | 1890 | 1895 | 1900 | 1905 | 1910 | 1915 | 1920 | 1925 | 1930 | 1935 |

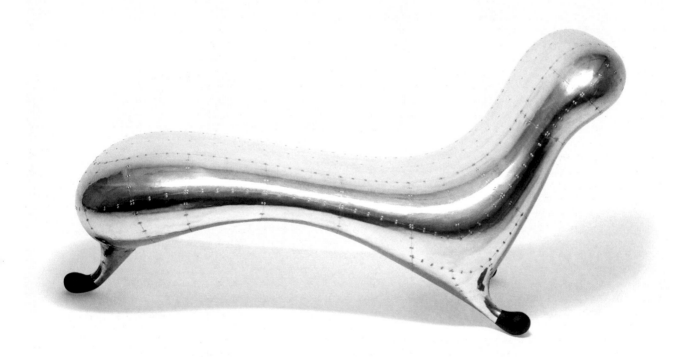

Marc Newson, Lockheed Lounge, 1986

MARC NEWSON

The award-winning Australian designer Marc Newson is known for his futuristic but technically sophisticated handling of industrial design.

Marc Newson is one of the most influential designers of our time. His career is unparalleled, his products range from household objects, lamps, furniture, and clocks to car designs and complete business installations. Many of his objects have already attained cult status and are coveted collector's items in design museums around the world. His designs are considered to be futuristic, sexy, humorous, and original. They are already essential components of modern pop culture and appear in videos by Madonna and in current films, such as the Austin Powers series.

Marc Newson, who was born in Sydney in 1962, studied jewelry design and sculpture at the Sydney College of Art. From 1987 on, he lived in Tokyo for several years and worked there as a designer for the Idée company run by Teruo Kurosaki. Newson found international fame with the *Lockheed Lounge*. This sculptural piece of furniture was presented in 1986 at the Roslyn Oxley Gallery in Sydney. The core consists of polyester reinforced with fiberglass that is covered with a skin of riveted sheet aluminum. The chaise looks very similar to the external covering of old aeroplanes although the shape of the furniture is round and organic. Newson also found fame in Europe with an exhibition of his designs at the Milan Furniture Fair. In 1992, he left Tokyo and moved to Paris, the new center of design for the 21st century, where he worked for design companies such as Flos (lights) and Cappellini (furniture). For Cappellini, he created the *Orgone Chair*, which is modeled on the surfboards of his Australian homeland, the *Black Hole* table, the *Event Horizon Table*, and the *Felt Chair*, unique pieces of furniture whose organic anthropomorphic forms caused a sensation. Larger orders for restaurant furnishings, for example Coast in London (1995) and Komed in Cologne (1996), gave Newson the chance to implement his visions in detail and to fully apply his organic technoid designs. With the design for a perfume bottle for Shiseido, Newson was finally able to afford his dream car, an Aston Martin DB4. Such sleek fashion cars still have a significant influence on Newson's designs, as do the film sets by Ken Adams for fantasy films and the models for space rockets.

In the mid-1990s, Newson met the computer genius Benjamin De Haan, who became his business partner. With the help of his new software, Newson was finally also able to design and realize larger design projects. In 1997, Newson and De Haan established a design studio in London, where Newson accepted two new dream projects: the design for the inside cabin of the Falcon 900B long-haul jet and the design for a Ford model, the 021C (1999–2000). With this concept car, Newson combined everything that he had accomplished in design up until now, from the shape of the car to the lovingly planned details of the interior fittings: seats that swivel on a pedestal, a sparkling, organically curved dashboard with instrument dials that resemble his Ikepod clocks, a steering wheel based on an Alessi coat hanger, carpets that resemble the shape of the *Orgone Chair*, and a roof that could be illuminated to bathe the interior in a snow-white light.

Like Philippe Starck, Marc Newson is today one of the superstars of design and he creates successful and exciting designs for many large, well-known companies such as Alessi, Magis, Boucheron, Dom Perignon, and the Quantas airline with such varied products as hairdryers, champagne bottles, coat hangers, door stops, lights, clocks (in his own company Ikepod), and even airplane seats. *hd*

1963 Born in Sydney, Australia
1982–84 Studies jewelry design and architecture at Sydney College of Art
1986 Exhibits the *Lockheed Lounge* at the Roslyn Oxley Gallery in Sydney
1989 Moves to Tokyo, designs for the Idée company run by Teruo Kurosaki, which produces the *Orgone Chair*, *Super Guppy Light* (1987), *Black Hole table* (1988), and the *Wicker Chair* (1990)
1992 New design studio in Paris
1997 Moves to London with his partner, Benjamin De Haan
1999 Presentation of the 021C concept car for Ford at the Tokyo Automobile Show
2002 Designs airplane seats for Quantas
2011 Lucky Strike Designer Award
2012 Awarded the CBE for his designs

Portrait of Marc Newson

MN Bicycle, Biomega, 1999

021C concept car, Ford Motor Co., 1999

1916–1922 Dadaist
movement

1850	1855	1860	1865	1870	1875	1880	1885	1890	1895	1900	1905	1910	1915	1920	1925	1930	1935

Joep van Lieshout, Floating Sculpture,
Atelier Van Lieshout, 2000

2004 Islamist terrorist attacks in Spain (March 11)

1939–1945 World War II **1969** Woodstock festival **1998** Construction of international space station (ISS) begins

1991 Damien Hirst, *The Physical Impossibility of*
1952 Samuel Beckett, **1973** Pablo Picasso dies *Death in the Mind of Someone Living* **2010** Catastrophic forest fires
Waiting for Godot in Russia

1940 1945 1950 1955 1960 1965 1970 1975 1980 1985 1990 1995 2000 2005 2010 2015 2020 2025

JOEP VAN LIESHOUT

Over the last ten years, Joup van Lieshout has created a compelling and complex range of works that are at the intersection of art, architecture, and design.

The accessible objects and mobile modules created by the Atelier van Lieshout collective, which was founded in 1995 by the Dutch artist Joep van Lieshout, cross the borders between applied and fine art. In an ironic way, they question the purpose and aesthetics of sculptures in the public arena. Amorphous and organoid structures dealing with the themes of housing, nutrition, waste disposal, locomotion, reproduction, and other physical functions form the core of his innovative artistic work.

It all began in 1988 with a series of furniture items made of polyester and designed by the graduate of the Rotterdam Academy. They are slightly reminiscent of Ikea furniture: workpieces based on standard dimensions that can be combined as required. In their reduced square form with the elementary primary color system, they evoke the art of the De Stijl movement and minimal art. However, more important than these references is the material polyester, which does not pretend to be anything other than what it is: hard-wearing and washable plastic. Polyester offered van Lieshout, who expanded the program to bathroom fittings from 1990 on, the maximum possible artistic freedom and at the same time is a lot cheaper than other materials such as wood or metal. With their lurid painting and haptic finish, these objects far exceed functional design and also evoke erotic associations.

In 1995, the artist founded the Atelier Van Lieshout (AVL) and expanded his production activity to larger installations and the "Mobile Modules." Old trailers and caravans were rebuilt as luxurious but sometimes also monstrous-looking living units that were used to travel across Europe and parked at international exhibitions (*Modular House Mobile*, 1995/96). The mobile modules were also given an architectural accent in the *Mobile Home for Kröller Müller* (1995), which consists of one master unit that can be expanded with various individual modules,

the slave units. While the master unit itself is an empty, wood-clad, mobile space, the function rooms – bathroom, bedroom, kitchen, and living area – are linked to the main room via the window openings. This creates a mobile two-room residence that, with its additive structure, resembles the container buildings on large building sites.

In addition to these extensive living, pleasure, and survival rooms, Joep van Lieshout also created "skulls," such as the *Sensory Deprivation Skull*, the *Study Book Skull*, and the *Bird Skull*. These are small containers like monks' cells, which with optimum architectural use of the interior space offer an opportunity to withdraw from the loud world and pursue spiritual activities. In these spatial situations, van Lieshout applies both the orgone theory of Wilhelm Reich as well as the SexPol movement, which was also initiated by Reich and which attempts to bring the theories of Karl Max into harmony with those of Sigmund Freud.

Van Lieshout's activities culminated in 2001 with the establishment of the city state "AVL-Ville" in the Rotterdam port area. However, this project, which considered itself to be a "provocative counterproject to state domination," was not tolerated by the authorities for long. With his large, room-filling installations (*The Technocrat*, 2004; *The Disciplinator*, 2005), Lieshout again raises questions of usefulness, aesthetics, and domination in order to simultaneously offer solutions for a new autonomous social structure. *hd*

1963 Born in Ravenstein, the
Netherlands
1980–85 Academy of Modern
Art Rotterdam
1985–87 Ateliers '63, Haarlem
1987 Villa Arson, Nice
FROM 1988 ON Polyester furniture
FROM 1992 ON Mobile Modules
1995 Establishes the artist collective
Atelier Van Lieshout (AVL)
2001 Establishes the city state
"AVL-Ville" in the Rotterdam
port area; prohibited by the
authorities and removed

Portrait of Joep van Lieshout

Fossil chairs, 2009

Hard Edge, 1989

1930 Luis Buñuel,
L'Age d'Or

1850 1855 1860 1865 1870 1875 1880 1885 1890 1895 1900 1905 1910 1915 1920 1925 1930 1935

1941 Bruce Nauman is born **1955–1968** Civil rights movement in the US **1983** Civil war breaks out in Sudan **1991** Conflict breaks out in the Balkans **2010** Mass panic at the Love Parade in Duisburg, Germany

1965 Beginning of Vietnam War **1986** Jeff Koons, *Rabbit* **1999** Columbine High School massacre

2005 Founding of YouTube

| 1940 | 1945 | 1950 | 1955 | 1960 | 1965 | 1970 | 1975 | 1980 | 1985 | 1990 | 1995 | 2000 | 2005 | 2010 | 2015 | 2020 | 2025 |

KONSTANTIN GRCIC

Konstantin Grcic is one of the most influential new designers from Germany. His futuristic designs are precisely thought out and constructed.

Konstantin Grcic designs a wealth of industrial products that can be called essential, simple, and even minimalist. Personally, he prefers the term "simplicity." His design philosophy is based on a mixture of formal severity, intellectual ingenuity, and a certain ironic twisting of material requirements. Functions are laid bare, structures made visible, and yet a sense for aesthetic and balance is still maintained. Grcic's design solutions are often experimental in the combination of materials and in their functional use, but they are always well thought out. The sources of his creativity are the constant dialog with industry, as well as the intensive conflict with the manufacture and the function of objects. In his designs, new technologies and ecological compatibility play as important a role as references to historical designs, for example to the aesthetics of Bauhaus.

Konstantic Grcic, who was born Munich in 1965, first completed a course in furniture making at Parnham College in England. He then studied design at the Royal College of Art in London from 1988 to 1990, and worked for a short time as the assistant to Jasper Morrison. He was stranded by chance in the not particularly uptown but creative train station district of Munich, where he has had his own office since 1991. On a return journey to London, the half-Serb with a Yugoslav passport was prevented from entering the country because he was not an EU citizen, and was sent back to where he had come from, to his grandmother in Munich. As a city, Munich does not really inspire him, but he and his employees can work there undisturbed, in his loft in Schillerstrasse. During the first ten years, Grcic – trained in the aesthetics of the Bauhaus school – preferred a more rational, strict design that works with austere, simple structures. Until now, his greatest design has been the *One* chair, which looks like a mathematical equation that can be sat on. The open frame, made of metal bars, can be painted in many colors and rests on a concrete base. Although

it was intended only for German open spaces, the rudimentary seat today appears in many European cities. *Mayday*, a robust pendant lamp with a plastic shade, also looks as if it belonged in a DIY hardware store.

Grcic's designs are just as stark as they are functional and are not without a humoristic note. The *Diana* side table from 2002 consists of only one vertical and two horizontal metal plates and yet it still has its own industrial charm. The *Tip* garbage can from 2003, whose lift mechanism for the lid is simply placed on the outside, is made entirely of plastic. In contrast, the *Table B* coffee table is an aluminum construction that looks like an airplane wing and rests on two trestles.

As simple as the designs appear, all products run through a defined sequence of processing steps before they are constructed. First, a pencil sketch is created and converted into a foam or paper model, then the fine details are completed on a computer, and finally a modelling form is developed for the finished product.

Design is not a mass product for Grcic, nor is it an elitist art concept. "Design is not art, but good design can have the quality of a piece of art. This can also be said of his chair. First of all it is pure design, but it also has a quality that far exceeds the fact that it is just a chair. So a plastic chair suddenly becomes an icon like a sculpture." (Konstantin Grcic)

Many of Konstantin Grcic's products have won international designer prizes (including Compasso d'Oro, 2001) and today form part of the permanent collections of some of the most famous museums, such as the Museum of Modern Art in New York and the Centre Georges Pompidou in Paris. The Royal Society for the Arts has named Konstantin Grcic Royal Designer for Industry. In 2010, he became a Fellow of the Villa Massimo in Rome. He also received the Designer of the Year Award from the Design Miami design fair in 2010. *hd*

1965 Born in Munich
1985 Moves to England; carpentry course at Parnham College, Dorset
1988–90 Studies design at the Royal College of Art, London
1991 Returns to Munich; opens his own design studio KGID (Konstantin Grcic Industrial Design)
1998 *Mayday* lamp for Flos
1999 Designs a porcelain range for Nymphenburg
2003 Designs the *One* chair range for Magis
2004 Start of collaboration with Krups for kitchen appliances
2007 Participates in the exhibition *25/25 – Celebrating 25 Years of Design* at the Design Museum, London

left page
Konstantin Grcic, One outdoor chair, 2004

above
Portrait of Konstantin Grcic

above
Pallas table, 2003

right page
Mayday lamp, 1998

1930 Grant Wood,
American Gothic

Edward Barber/Jay Osgerby,
Loop Table

1944 Normandy landings

1956 Elvis Presley has his first
major hit, *Heartbreak Hotel*

1949 The Soviet Union commences
its first atomic test

1962 Andy Warhol, *Campbell's Soup Cans*

1973 First commercial personal computer

1981 Ronald Reagan sworn in as
40th president of the US

1969 Stonewall riots on Christopher Street in New York

1990 End of Cold War

2003 US invasion of Iraq

2009 Swine flu epidemic

| 1940 | 1945 | 1950 | 1955 | 1960 | 1965 | 1970 | 1975 | 1980 | 1985 | 1990 | 1995 | 2000 | 2005 | 2010 | 2015 | 2020 | 2025 |

EDWARD BARBER & JAY OSGERBY

School chairs that tilt, torches for Olympia, tiles for Stella McCartney, and a clothes hook for Levi's – designs by BarberOsgerby are as diverse as they are original. The British design duo Jay Osgerby and Edward Barber have worked at the intersection of industrial design, furniture design, and architecture since their university days.

Edward Barber and Jay Osgerby met during their postgraduate studies at the Royal College of Art in London and from then on started their careers as part of the design elite. After they graduated, they immediately set up the design studio BarberOsgerby and won great acclaim for their first project together, the *Loop Table* (1997), which they presented at the London exhibition "100% Design." The Italian furniture manufacturer Giulio Cappellini so admired the table, which was originally designed for a restaurant, that he started to manufacture it immediately. This fortunate encounter led to a collaboration that would last for many years.

In addition to the *Loop Table*, other classic BarberOsgerby designs include the *Tab* light and the *Tip Ton* chair. The *Tab* light was developed as an extension of the classic drawing table light as the drawing table was also ultimately replaced by the computer. It is multifunctional and can be used on a desk as well as on a bedside table or as a couch reading lamp. The *Tip Ton* chairs were developed as part of a project to improve schoolroom furnishings. These simple, two-level chairs were designed to enable schoolchildren to sit without being restricted and to be able to move more freely.

However, to reduce Edward Barber and Jay Osgerby to individual design objects would be too limiting. Since setting up their (interior) architecture agency "Universal Design Studio" in particular, the two designers have also realized complete room concepts. Their most extensive works include the interior design of the former Battersea Power Station in London, which was converted into apartments and industrial units.

The duo achieved popularity through cooperating with famous names, which enabled them to prove their creativity and versatility over and over again. They designed tiles for Stella McCartney's shop in New York, an exhibition room for Damien Hirst, innovative clothes hooks for Levi jeans, glass vases for Murano glass, and a sound experience room for Sony – the list goes on and on.

In spite of their versatility, the style of BarberOsgerby can be described in their own words as "exercise in reduction." With their designs, the pair want to use existing materials and to use working practices in a new and more intelligent way, thus avoiding unnecessary details. For example, in their early years, they developed existing laminate wood techniques. Later, they concentrated more on colors and created a completely new approach to design using color as the starting point. Colorful examples are the *Iris* table (2009), which is devoted to a particular color spectrum and depicts this spectrum in a circle.

The design duo received an accolade in 2005 when they were selected to modernize the seating in the De La Warr pavilion for its anniversary. Seventy years before, none other than Alvar Aalto had designed the chairs for the pavilion. *nk*

1969 Edward Barber is born in
Shrewsbury, Great Britain,
Jay Osgerby in Oxford, Great
Britain

1996 They graduate in architecture
from the Royal College of Art in
London

1996 They establish the design agency
BarberOsgerby in the Trellick
Tower in London

1997 *Loop Table*

1998 ICFF Editors Award: Best New
Designer

2001 They establish the architecture
agency "Universal Design Studio"

2006 "Designers of the Future" award

2007 *Blueprint* magazine award
"Product of the Year"; red dot
award

2009 Commission from Murano Glas

2010 Sound experience room for Sony;
Design of the Olympic torch for
the 2012 Olympic Games in
London

Portrait of Barber & Osgerby

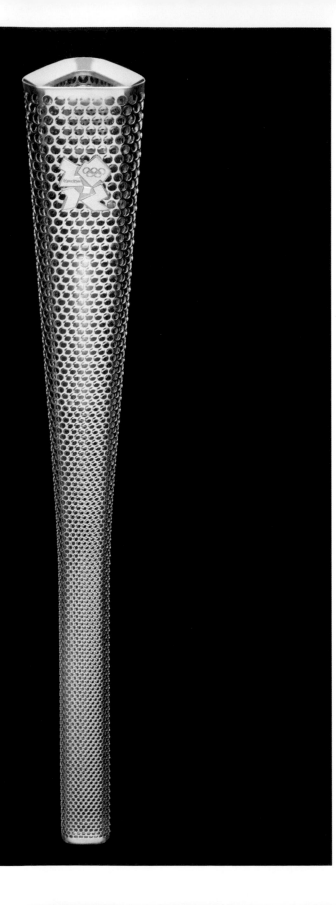

left
Olympic torch designed for the
Olympic Games 2012 in London

right page
Tip Ton chairs, 2011

1931 Second Span
Republic
proclaimed ir
Madrid

1929 Stock market
crash heralds
global economic
crisis

1850	1855	1860	1865	1870	1875	1880	1885	1890	1895	1900	1905	1910	1915	1920	1925	1930	1935	

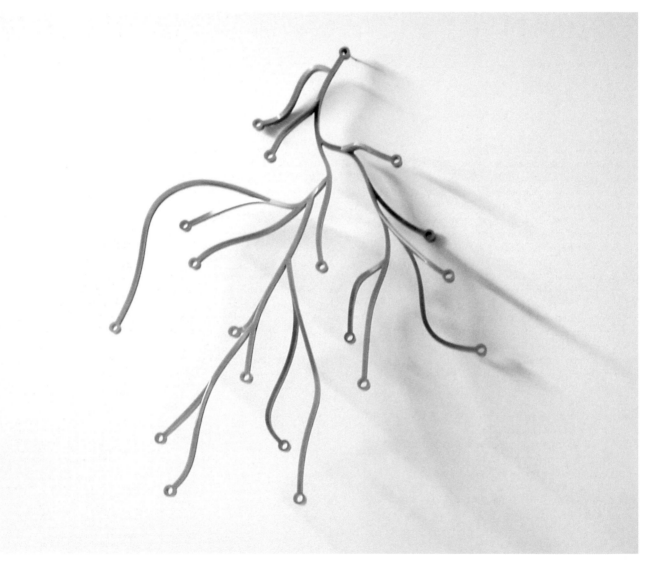

Ronan and Erwan Bouroullec,
Algues, 2004

1960 Clement Greenberg, *Modernist Painting*

1973 US Supreme Court legalizes abortion

2001 Apple iPod launched

1993 Bombay bombings

1964 Racial segregation abolished in the US

1986 First modular space station *Mir*; *Challenger* space shuttle disaster

1940 Trotsky murdered in Mexico

2007 Al Gore awarded Nobel Peace Prize

| 1940 | 1945 | 1950 | 1955 | 1960 | 1965 | 1970 | 1975 | 1980 | 1985 | 1990 | 1995 | 2000 | 2005 | 2010 | 2015 | 2020 | 2025 |

RONAN & ERWAN BOUROULLEC

The Bouroullec brothers are amongst the best-known contemporary designers. Although many of their organically inspired projects initially appear to be artistic experiments, they are in fact planned in detail and are sensitively tailored to the needs of people.

Their early discovery by Giulio Cappellini at the Salone Internazionale del Mobile furniture fair in Milan in 1997 says much about the duo's extraordinary talent. The constructive dialogue of the different viewpoints of the brothers, their ambitious perfectionism, as well as their vision of furniture, which responds to the human condition, have given them a successful career. With their own combination of organic structures and a high level of technical understanding, during their career, they have created the Paris showroom for fashion designer Issey Miyake and have also carried out many projects for the designer furnishing giant Vitra. A striking example is the *Vegetal* chair from 2008, which is inspired by the growth of plants yet still has a completely autonomous impact.

The designs by the brothers, who are five years apart in age, are characterized by balance, empathy, and an attention to detail that verges on tenacity. Ronan, the older of the two, was born in 1971, Erwan in 1976. After Ronan graduated from the École nationale supérieure des arts décoratifs in Paris in 1996, he opened his own studio immediately and began to work. His brother, who was still studying, assisted him on some projects until he also received his diploma from the École nationale supérieure d'arts in Cergy-Pontoise and became a partner. After their success at the Milan furniture fair and projects such as the *Spring Chair* with Capellini (1997), the young designers were noticed by Rolf Fehlbaum, the owner of Vitra, in 2000. This contact was the start of a highly successful collaboration, the first product of which was the *Joyn* office furniture system, which is still being constantly expanded today. This was followed by *Algues* (2004), a transparent room separation solution for offices, the harmonious *Worknest* swivel chair (2006), the intimate *Alcove* sofa (2006) with its head-high backrest, and the injection-molded chair *Vegetal* (2008). However, the Bouroullecs do not just design for Vitra; their studio also works on diverse furniture and architectural

projects. They also created the *Steelwood* and *Stripped* series for the Italian manufacturer Magis. In 2006, they collaborated with the Centre National de l'estampe et de l'art imprimé, who wanted to build a floating pavilion for guest authors to the center. With their usual finesse, the Bouroullecs created and furnished the Floating House. The floor of the houseboat was so close to the waterline that the visitors felt that they were walking on water.

The impressive catalog of successes based on their extensive conflict with both the functional and the poetical made the Bouroullecs known outside the design scene, and each new project is awaited by the public with anticipation. The brothers perfect their interior design and production concepts to the smallest detail and, unlike many designers, they focus on subtle human sensations. *jr*

1971 Ronan Bouroullec is born in Quimper
1976 Erwan Bouroullec is born in Quimper
1996 Ronan graduates from the École nationale supérieure des arts décoratifs in Paris; sets up a design agency
1997 Presentation of *Disintegrated Kitchen* at the Milan furniture fair, first industrial commissions
1999 Erwan completes his studies at the École nationale supérieure d'arts in Cergy-Pontoise; partner in his brother's agency
2000 Commission to create the showroom for the A-Poc fashion collection by Issy Miyake in Paris, start of the long-term collaboration with Vitra
2001–11 Various experimental design projects, which are presented to the public at four exhibitions at the Galerie Kreon in Paris
SINCE 2004 Designs for the Italian furniture manufacturer Magis
2006 Architectural project *Floating House*
2011 Designer of the Year Award for Now! Maison & Objet in Paris

Portrait of Ronan and Erwan Bouroullec

Alcove, 2006

Worknest, 2006

1925 Invention of
television

| 1850 | 1855 | 1860 | 1865 | 1870 | 1875 | 1880 | 1885 | 1890 | 1895 | 1900 | 1905 | 1910 | 1915 | 1920 | 1925 | 1930 | 1935 |

Apple, iPod classic

1939–1945 World War II

1966 Barnett Newman, *Who's Afraid of Red, Yellow and Blue*

1975 Pol Pot comes to power in Cambodia

1983 Civil war breaks out in Sudan

1985 Live Aid concert for Africa

1995 *Toy Story* is first movie produced entirely with computer animation

2001 First same-sex "marriage" in Holland

2007 iPhone launched

1940 1945 1950 1955 1960 1965 1970 1975 1980 1985 1990 1995 2000 2005 2010 2015 2020 2025

APPLE – JONATHAN IVE

It is simplicity that drives him. No gimmicks, no frills, not a single superfluous button. The products should be elegant and intuitive to use. They should have style. We are of course talking about Apple products: the iPod, iMac, iPhone, and iPad. Their success is down to Steve Jobs, who died at too young an age. However, neither Jobs nor his successor, Tim Cook, were behind for the design of Apple products. Since 1997, it has been down to a British man: Jonathan Ive.

When Jobs was alive, Ive was one of his closest colleagues at Apple. In 1997, when Jobs returned to the company, which was in crisis at that time, he was so impressed by Ive's studies that he put him in charge of design. It is even said that Jobs told the company that: "No one can tell him what to do." There couldn't have been a greater recognition of Ive's work for, as well as his flair, Jobs was also known for his company credo: "Apple, that is me." And Jonathan Ive, who was born in northeast London in 1967 and first worked for a British design company, repaid Jobs's appreciation. After becoming the head of design at Apple, he created design icons that sold in their millions.

One product, however, stands out from Ive's design oeuvre because it is so different. It was, nevertheless, Ive's first success: the candy-colored iMacs from the late 1990s. They already showed what Ive and Apple considered to be important: they emotionalize their products, load them with values. An Apple product is purchased because it is attractive and valuable.

Jonathan Ive, who lives in San Fransisco, said in an interview with the BBC: "There is beauty when something works and it works intuitively." He thus falls into line with the Braun designer Dieter Rams and his "Ten Rules for Good Design," which included: "Good design makes a product understandable." When talking about Ive's work, Rams once said that Apple was one of the few companies who still worked according to his ten rules.

Ive's homage to Ram's pragmatic aesthetics and his reduced designs can be clearly recognized in one particular product that accelerated Apple's rise at the start of the new century. The pocket transistor radio T3 from 1958 with its characteristic rotary wheel served as a blueprint for the Apple MP3 player. Forty years later, Ive designed the first generation iPod as a legitimate successor to the Braun device, including the scroll wheel. With the iPod, Ive thus designed a product that turned the

music industry on its head. Ive's newer products, the iPad and the iPhone, are also based on the iPod design, and they were partly responsible for setting a new standard in the mobile telephone and computer industry.

By this time, the rather shy and retiring Ive was one of the most important contemporary product designers on the planet, although he himself says: "People's interest is in the product, not the authorship." The Queen of England sees this rather differently. She recently honored Ive with a knighthood for his outstanding contribution to design and entrepreneurship. So Jonathan Ive has indeed made a new name for himself. The latest is: Sir Jonathan. *mm*

1967 Born in Chingford, a suburb of London
1987 Marries Heather Pegg
1989 Graduates with a degree in industrial design from Newcastle Polytechnic Art School in the northeast of England
1992 Employed by Apple
1997 Steve Jobs returns to Apple; the iMac goes into production a short time later. Since then, Ive has been lead designer at the company
2001 Presentation of the iPod designed by Ive
2011 Awarded an honorary knighthood (KBE) by Queen Elizabeth II

Jonathan Ive lives in San Francisco

left
Apple, iPad

above
Apple Store in New York

1850 1855 1860 1865 1870 1875 1880 1885 1890 1895 1900 1905 1910 1915 1920 1925 1930 1935

1965 Beginning of Vietnam War
1999 Columbine High School massacre
1941 Bruce Nauman is born **1955–1968** Civil rights movement in the US
1986 Jeff Koons, *Rabbit* **2005** Founding of YouTube
1970 Willy Brandt's Warsaw
Ghetto genuflection
1991 Conflict breaks out
in the Balkans
2010 Mass panic at the Love Parade
in Duisburg, Germany

1940   1945   1950   1955   1960   1965   1970   1975   1980   1985   1990   1995   2000   2005   2010   2015   2020   2025

MUJI

"Muji is good for you," claimed the British product designer Jasper Morrison in 2003.
The Japanese chain of lifestyle department stores with their non-branded products combines quality and functionality
with minimalist design at a reasonable price.

Founded in 1980 in Japan, Muji sees itself as a critical response to the consumer behavior influenced by the economic boom of the time. The market was defined by the popularity of foreign luxury brands as a status symbol on the one hand and low-quality, cheap, no-name products on the other.

The company name "mu jirushi ryô hin" (consisting of four Japanese characters in the corporate color, bordeaux) and abbreviated as Muji, literally means "no brand, good products." The focus here is just the high-quality product, not the label, and the customer should be attracted by the favorable price/quality ratio. The careful choice of material, environmentally and resource-friendly manufacturing processes, and elegant packaging also play an important role.

"Less is more when you are creating something very simple," explains Kenya Hara, creative director at Muji. The concept of "reduction to the bare minimum" is apparent in both the design and the communication and restrained presentation of the products. Muji articles are characterized by a standard and subtle color palette and clear minimalistic shapes with a focus on simple functionality. The interior architecture of the Muji stores is strictly purist and consists mainly of shelves and tables made of wood, glass, or steel. With the exception of catalogs, posters, and specific advertisement campaigns, there is no extensive advertising. At the same time, with this philosophy, Muji connects with the Japanese ideal of "shibui" (*elegant, subtle, simple, natural*), a key concept of Japanese aesthetics.

Although many products were designed by international designers such as Naoto Fukasawa, Enzo Mari, Jasper Morrison, Konstantin Grcic, Sam Hecht, Shin and Tomoko Azumi, the designers also remain anonymous in accordance with the "no brand" approach. The Japanese company has won numerous design prizes, including five "iF Product

Design Gold Awards" from the International Forum Design in Germany (2005) and the "Good Design Award Japan." One of most successful and best-known examples, the wall CD player by Naoto Fukasawa/IDEO Japan, is part of the collection at the Museum of Modern Art in New York. *aw*

1980 Founded as the house brand for the Seiyu Ltd department store with 40 everyday items (nine household items and 31 grocery items)
1981 Expansion of the range to include stationery and textiles
1983 Opening of the first direct Muji branch in Aoyama, Tokyo
1989 Muji becomes independent from Seiyu Ltd.
1991 Opening of the first Muji branch abroad (London)
2003 World Muji Project: increased collaboration with international designers
2006 "Muji Award 01," first international design competition
2012 Represented in 20 countries with 509 retail outlets and over 6,000 products from groceries and stationery to household and hygiene articles to clothing, furniture, and electronic applicances
In Japan there are also Muji household and entertainment electronics, Muji florists, Muji opticians, Muji cafes, Muji kiosks, Muji campsites, and Muji houses.

left page
Muji, Wall CD radio by Naoto Fukasawa

above
Wall CD player-radio remote control

1850 1855 1860 1865 1870 1875 1880 1885 1890 1895 1900 1905 1910 1915 1920 1925 1930 1935

Display in the Swatch store in Zurich, 2007

1945 Auschwitz concentration camp
liberated on January 27

1969 Woodstock festival

2004 Islamist terrorist attacks in Spain (March 11)

1998 Construction of international space station (ISS) begins

1939–1945 World War II

1973 Pablo Picasso dies

1991 Damien Hirst, *The Physical Impossibility of
Death in the Mind of Someone Living*

1952 Samuel Beckett,
Waiting for Godot

1984 Civil war breaks out in Sudan

2010 Catastrophic forest fires
in Russia

1940　1945　1950　1955　1960　1965　1970　1975　1980　1985　1990　1995　2000　2005　2010　2015　2020　2025

SWATCH

From the "impossible" watch to the "inevitable" sales success: swatch *transformed the watch from a device for measuring time into a fashionable accessory.*

In the 1970s, cheap Asian digital watches were forcing high-quality Swiss chronometers from the market, plunging the local watch industry into a serious crisis. In Switzerland, around half of the 120,000 employees in this sector lost their jobs within five years. There was a feverish search for an option to serve the lower price segment.

The first audacious solution finally came from the Grench clockworks factory ETA SA. In March 1980, the director, Ernst Thomke, received a request to buy an injection-molding machine for more than half a million Swiss francs. The request came from the plastic technologist Elmar Mock, who, together with the mechanic Jacques Müller, had developed a radical concept to produce a plastic-based watch and needed the machine for his experiments.

Enraged, Thomke summoned Mock to his office, but when he saw the rough sketches of the plastic watch, he recognized their appeal. The first design contained a plastic housing from one mold into which the basic clockworks and the clock face were set and permanently welded together with a Perspex cover to make it waterproof. The robust watch was worn on a plastic strap and, unusually, built up from the lower side to the upper side. This enabled automated production that was much more cost effective than manual assembly. In addition, the plastic permitted adventurous color combinations, which were perfectly suited to the extrovert 1980s.

Mock and Müller were allowed to develop the prototypes with the utmost secrecy and Franz Sprecher became responsible for the marketing concept: they were to be marketed as a fun accessory and under their own brand, which would be completely separate from the "timeless" and costly chronometers. The fact that this idea had the potential to help the entire sector to get back on its feet again was recognized by Nicolas George Hayek. At the time, the business consultant was working on the restructuring of the SMH SA mother group and he now approved additional funds to quickly launch the project. He also devised the name for the new brand: the fast-moving watch was to be called *swatch*, a combination of "second" and "watch."

In 1982, the first 10,000 *swatch* watches were delivered to the US as a test, but they were unpopular with customers owing to the uninspiring colors. Only when the idea of creating half-yearly collections was introduced and the Zurich designers Robert & Durrer reworked the design of the watch was a completely integrated concept created. The impossible plastic watch became an individual fashion accessory and a sensational commercial success. Thanks to automated production, in 1984, one year after the launch in Switzerland, the millionth *swatch* was manufactured and this number grew to 3.5 million in the same year.

This led to cooperation with artists such as Mimmo Paladino, Kiki Picasso, and Keith Haring, who each designed a *swatch* collection. The watches, originally very trendy and designed for young people, became more attractive to an older audience and a collection culture quickly developed around the cult watch. It became the most important flagship product for the restructured SMH SA, which had changed its name to The Swatch Group Ltd in 1998, and helped the entire Swiss watch industry to develop a young, fresh image. Other projects launched in the wake of this success included the concept for the small city car *smart* and in the 1990s, Swatch even briefly tried to introduce a new time concept called "beats."

Although the popularity of the *swatch* reached its climax in the 1980s, it is still a popular accessory and Swatch has also become the sponsor for various extreme sports. The Swatch Group's product range is constantly being expanded and the models from the collection of *swatch* originals are almost too numerous to count. As before, the group has ambitious plans for its flagship brand: by 2033, they plan to sell the 1,111 millionth of the colorful watches that saved the Swiss watch industry. *jr*

1980 Elmar Mock and Jacques Müller develop the concept of a low-cost and fashion-based plastic watch at the clockworks factory ETA SA

1983 The *swatch* is launched on the market

1984 The 3.5 millionth *swatch* is produced

1990 At an auction, a model from the special collection by the artist Mimmo Paladino fetches a price of 56,000 Swiss francs

1990s Swatch tries to establish other products under the brand *swatch*, but the attempts fail

1992 The 100 millionth *swatch* is sold

1994 Swatch expands its catalog to include a range in metal, *Irony*

1998 SMH SA changes its name to the Swatch Group

2006 The 333 millionth *swatch* is sold

2010 Nicolas G. Hayek dies, his daughter is elected to the supervisory board of the Swatch Group

1850 1855 1860 1865 1870 1875 1880 1885 1890 1895 1900 1905 1910 1915 1920 1925 1930 1935

Droog (Jurgen Bey), Tree-trunk bench

1965 Joseph Beuys action: "How to explain pictures to a dead hare"

1992 Founding of the European Union

2010 Mass panic at the Love Parade in Duisburg, Germany

1948/49 Berlin Airlift

1982 Michael Jackson, *Thriller*

2005 Founding of YouTube

1939 Germany invades Poland; World War II commences

1973 Chilean coup d'état; elected president Salvador Allende dies

1999 Columbine High School massacre

| 1940 | 1945 | 1950 | 1955 | 1960 | 1965 | 1970 | 1975 | 1980 | 1985 | 1990 | 1995 | 2000 | 2005 | 2010 | 2015 | 2020 | 2025 |

DROOG DESIGN

With their sharp ideas, the Dutch designer group Droog Design have been causing a stir for years. Luxury is not a question of money or precious materials; it is the sole result of thoughtful ideas.

Droog Design ("droog" is Dutch for "dry") is an internationally renowned Dutch designer collective located in Amsterdam. Droog Design develops and produces furniture, lamps, accessories, and objects. Many internationally well-known designers work for Droog, including Marcel Wanders, Hella Jongerius, Tejo Remy, Richard Hutten, and Jurgen Bey. Some products from the company can also be seen in important international design collections, for example in the Museum of Modern Art in New York (MoMA) and in the Central Museum of Utrecht.

The 1980s can be considered both the peak of postmodern design as well as a low point in design history. Lamps had ornamental protuberances, furniture took the form of body parts, and the Alessi teapot had a golden metal lid with a knob that could burn fingers. Then at the start of the 1990s, a movement surfaced that confronted ostentatious everyday design with a provocative dryness: Droog Design was founded in 1993 by Gijs Baker and the design historian Renny Ramakers with the aim of opposing the prevailing formally playful and elite understanding of design with a conceptual, pragmatic but often also subjective and rugged design. At the Milan Furniture Fair of 1993 the founders of Droog Design presented objects from young Dutch designers that were like aesthetic explosions among the artistic offshoots of 1980s' designs: a bookshelf made of strips of brown paper, and Tejo Remy's "Multiplex," a chest of drawers that consisted of nothing but old drawers held together by a jute band – a crude mixture of the pioneer spirit of the early Ikea boxes and the improvisation-ready junk creativity of the 1960s. Droog Design did not create a new style but instead they developed a new attitude whereby postmodernist gimmicks were accompanied by a new objectivity and also dry humor. Since then, the Dutch designers have frequently presented their products at fairs and in renowned design stores and they generate at least a few smiles when, for example, a tree trunk is fitted with antique armrests

and thus becomes an aesthetically memorable piece of furniture – albeit not the most comfortable.

Last but not least, the products from Droog live on the idea of recycling: for example, twelve empty milk bottles are provided with lightbulbs and bundled together into a minimalist sculpture (Tejo Remy). Such associations are reminiscent both of the Ready-Made movement of Marcel Duchamp and the everyday culture of pop. The seat made of rags, held together by packaging tape, belongs in the repertoire of the design factory, which now works with over 100 independent designers throughout the world.

Since 2004, the designer duo has had its offices in an old factory building in Amsterdam. There is a shop, a showroom, a library, and a kitchen in which events are held. Droog Design sends its products throughout the world from Amsterdam and today is one of the most recognized international design labels with over 180 products in the categories of light and lighting, furniture, kitchen, bathroom, tabletop, and accessories. *hd*

1942 Gijs Bakker is born on February 20 in Amsterdam

1993 Establishes Droog Design together with Renny Ramakers; presentation of the first furniture items at the Milan Furniture Fair

1996 First cooperation with a company (dry tech)

2000 Own factory for designs in Amsterdam

2004 Droog Headquarters in Amsterdam; *Simply Droog. 10 + 1 Years Avant-garde Design from the Netherlands*, Haus der Kunst, Munich

Portrait of Droog

INDEX

PHOTO CREDITS

© Alessi: p. 86, 87, 88, 89
© Alessi/Carlo Lavatori: Frontispiece
Courtesy of Karim Rashid Inc.: p. 10/11
Thonet GmbH: p. 12 (Michael Gerlach), 13, 14 (Constantin Meyer), 15 (Michael Gerlach), p. 29
IAM/akg-images: p. 16, S. 31
akg-images: p. 19, 43
Cassina, Mailand (Mario Carrieri): p. 20, 34
TECTA, Lauenförde: p. 26, 28, 32, 52, 54, 55
Jacek Marczewski © 2003 The Museum of Modern Art, New York: 30
Bauhaus-Archiv, Berlin (photo: Gunter Lepkowski): p. 38
© Raymond Loewy Foundation, Hamburg: p. 40, 41/42 below
akg-images/Paul Almasy: p. 41 above
© Louis Poulsen: p. 44, 45
Artek: p. 46
Ensio Ilmonen and Lehtikuva: p. 47
Wilhelm Wagenfeld Stiftung, Bremen: S. 48
© Vitra: p. 22, 50, 51, 61, 108, 110/110
© Vitra/Andreas Sütterlin: p. 60, 74
© Vitra Collections AG: p. 62
© Fritz Hansen: p. 56, 57, 58, 59
© Eames Foundation: p. 63

© Manufactum (www.manufactum.de)
akg-images/Angelika Platen: p. 69
Mid Century Modern Gallery, Kapstadt: p. 66
akg-images/Tony Vaccaro: p. 67
Stedelijk Museum, Amsterdam: p. 68
Maaria Wirkkala: p. 69
Tapio Wirkkala Rut Bryk Foundation: p. 70, 71
Victoria and Albert Museum, London: p. 72
Alberto Fioravanti: p. 76
Barbara Radice Sottsass: p. 77
Memphis, Mailand: p. 78
Studio Ettore Sottsass srl: p. 79
Studio Museo Achille Castiglioni: p. 80
Mauro Galligani /laif: p. 81
Courtesy Studio Magistretti Archive - Vico Magistretti Foundation: p. 82, 83, 84, 85
Studio Putman: p. 90
Raphael DEMARET/REA/laif: p. 91
Verner Panton Design, Bern: p. 92, 93, 94, 95
Studio Conran: p. 96, 97, 98, 99
Procter & Gamble Germany: p. 100, 101
© Ingo Maurer: p. 102, 103, 104, 105
© Philippe Starck: p. 106
Thomas Bilanges: p. 107

Ron Arad Associates: p. 112, 113
Vitra/Hans Hansen: p. 109
Tom Dixon Studio: p. 114
Pierre Olivier Deschamps/VU/laif: p. 115
André Huber: p. 116
momoko Japan: p. 117
Courtesy of Karim Rashid Inc.: p. 118, 119, 120/121
Carin Katt: p. 122
Tom Vack: p. 125
Courtesy of Mark Newson Limited: p. 123, 156
Tue Schiorring: p. 124
© Atelier van Lieshout: p. 126, 128, 129
Merlijn Doomernik/Hollandse Hoogte/laif: p. 127
Konstantin Grcic Industrial Design: p. 130, 132, 133
Tibor Bozi: p. 131
© Ronan and Erwan Bouroullec: p. 138, 140, 141
© Ola Rindal: p. 139
© Edward Barber and Jay Osgerby: p. 134, 136, 137
© Linda Brownlee: p. 135
© 2012 Apple Inc.: p. 142, 143
© Muji: p. 144, 145
© Gaetan Bally/Keystone Schweiz/laif: p. 146
© Droog Design: p. 148, 149, 150, 151

TEXTS

Hajo Düchting (hd): 23, 35, 51, 61, 65, 77, 81, 91, 97, 119, 123, 127, 131, 149
Claudia Hellmann (ch): 13, 19, 25, 39, 41, 57, 63, 67, 69, 103
Nina Kozel (nk): 17, 27, 29, 31, 37, 45, 47, 53, 73, 87, 93, 107, 109, 115, 135
Marco Maurer (mm): 143
Johannes Rave (jr): 33, 75, 83, 101, 113, 139, 147
Josef Straßer (js): 49
Annette Winkler (aw): 117, 145